Carolann Dowding *grew up in the Redlands in the 1950s. She led a happy, privileged life until she was four, when her adoption was revealed. Over the ensuing years, curiosity about her birth family occupied a special place in her heart and in her early thirties she started a relentless search for her birth family.*

Carolann's memoir describes her childhood, documents her search and subsequent reunion with her birth mother, Edna, as an adult. Edna concealed the identity of Carolann's birth father until the truth was revealed years later.

In later life, Carolann changed her adoptive name 'Jean' to her original birth name, 'Carolann', provoking mixed reactions from her friends and family.

Digital Publishing Centre
Brisbane

Shadows in Paradise

A Memoir

Carolann Dowding

Digital Publishing Centre
Brisbane

The Digital Publishing Centre
an imprint of Interactive Publications
Treetop Studio • 9 Kuhler Court
Carindale, Queensland, Australia 4152
sales@ipoz.biz
ipoz.biz/DPC/DPC.htm

First published by IP in 2013
© Carolann Dowding, 2013

Printed in 11 pt Book Antiqua on 14 pt Book Antiqua.

National Library of Australia
Cataloguing-in-Publication entry:

Author: Dowding, Carolann, author.

Title: Shadows in paradise : a memoir / Carolann Dowding.

ISBN: 9781922120663 (paperback)

Subjects: Dowding, Carolann.
            Adoptees--Australia--Biography
            Birthparents--Australia--Identification.
            Adoptees--Australia--Family relationships.

Dewey Number: 362.8298092

Dedicated,
with love and gratitude,
to John
who took
the journey with me.

Acknowledgements

Cover Image: Bobby Gordon

Jacket Design: David P Reiter

Author Photo: Ray Rapinette

My grateful thanks to David Reiter and Lauren Daniels at Interactive Publications for their guidance and encouragement throughout the editing and publishing stage.

And thanks to my friends and family who read the raw manuscript, offered encouragement and issued helpful hints. Also thank you to everyone who helped search for elusive photo credits.

Contents

*Those who do not have power
over the story that dominates their lives,
power to retell it,
deconstruct it,
joke about it,
and change it as time changes,
truly are powerless,
because they cannot think new thoughts.*

Salman Rushdie

Poem from the Heart

Never be afraid to try something new.
Remember amateurs built the ark.
Professionals built the Titanic.

Wolfgang Riebe

2009

It is dark. My thoughts swirl. The digital clock reads 3.00am.
I fumble for the light switch, throw back the covers and climb
out of bed. I find a pen and paper and record my words.

Baby was born and sent on her way,
So innocent she had no say,
When her life changed on that fateful day.
'What might have been' held no sway,
As baby was tragically carried away.

When she was grown,
She trudged the mire,
To find mother, father,
Her heart's desire.

Her mother knows
It was a dreadful sin,
To give her own
For a stranger's kin.

With baby gone
her soul felt wrong.
Her heart was heavy,
She must move on,
Forever with an empty space,
Nothing new will ever replace.

Her heart is on fire,
She knows for sure,
When she was born
and life was poor,
No family celebrations
Passed through her door.

No blue and pink and lemon trims,
No cards and ribbons and lacy whims,
No flowers and toys and happy pics,
No nursery sets and building bricks.

Her father never held her hand,
Counted to ten,
Nor helped her stand.
Popped the cork and drank a toast,
Sent her flowers or did his most.

His heart is on fire,
He feels the cost,
He will never know the child he lost.
He will only know her in his mind
Society disapproves his kind.

Her heart is on fire,
the mind is a liar,
her spirit is full of strange desire,
Sorrow, anger, fear and strain,
'What might have been?'
Brings on the pain.

Her heart is on fire,
She is growing wings,
To fly above the hurtful things.
She questions which road she should take,
To try, deny or maybe break?

Her heart is on fire,
She would love to know,
How did they cleave,
Then let her go?
The answer nigh may not be true,
Where and when and why and who?

1

Miasma

When your mind is full of indecision,
try thinking with your heart.
– *Believe in Yourself Journal* by Heather Zschock, Sophia Bedford-Pierce & Beth Mende Conny

1950s

My adoptive mother, Mary, and I often examined the memorabilia contained in her camphor-wood chest and especially enjoyed looking at the baby clothes I had worn as a newborn. Although the garments were discoloured and faded, they retained their fragile beauty.

January 1982

I pressed my nose to the windowpane and observed the sky as it transformed into shades of orange and gold. My heart raced as shadows of the unknown beckoned me. Tonight I would cross a boundary. Tonight I would phone my birth mother.

I squinted through the glass and watched the darkness grow. Lights appeared in neighbouring houses as the blackness softened untidy grass and straggly hedges.

The season was high summer. My family had sweltered since dawn and dusk brought small relief. The broiling air was trapped in the ceiling and radiated a furnace-like invasion into the small rooms of the cottage.

I was aware only of my heartbeat as I twisted my clammy hands into contortions.

Without warning, a din echoed through the cottage. My husband glanced up at the ceiling and I realised it was only the pop and crackle of the iron roof as it retracted in the night air. I turned back to the window and pushed the frame upwards.

That night I had chosen to contact my birth mother for the first time since she relinquished me thirty-four years ago. Would I recognise her voice? Maybe. Incredulous as it sounds, a foetus can hear in the womb by the second trimester.

I was aware I spent my first ten days in the Brisbane Women's Hospital with my birth mother. Did she cuddle me, caress me and feed me? Perhaps I had repressed memories?

The bond between my birth mother and I was severed when I was two weeks old and the event would have devastated us both. Many studies have proven that babies know and recognise their mothers. Would I?

It is also acknowledged that when a baby and mother are permanently separated, the baby is traumatised. First, the foetus bonds with its mother physically, psychologically and spiritually, then the bonding continues after birth as the mother's scent, voice and face imprint upon the child. The act of feeding (breast or bottle) enhances the intimate relationship. After the separation from my birth mother, I would have experienced abandonment, and felt it stamped on my unconscious mind forever.

My thoughts returned to the oppressive atmosphere in the cottage. The atrocious heat wave did nothing to help my anxiety. Suddenly my mind infused with a state of derealisation; my eyes were unfocused; the room's perspective warped; my arms and legs felt like lead.

Despite the heat, our children slept. A rare but welcome puff of air ruffled the curtains and as the scent of frangipani wafted inside I visualised thousands of pink blossoms displayed in our garden and tried to focus.

The little cottage, situated on my adoptive parents' farm, was home for my husband, John, and our three children Christopher, Lachlan and Andrew while our home was under construction. My adoptive parents, Mary and Jack Gordon, lived three kilometres away in the old Queenslander where I grew up with my adoptive brother, Ian, who still lived there with them. I had the support of a loving family all around me. Why was I doing this?

I grabbed a notepad from the coffee table and noticed my sweaty hands had dampened the paper. I stared at the phone number. John, who had promised his support, waited patiently.

Ten minutes later John walked across to the sofa and plonked himself down.

I shuffled over and sat beside him. "I'll phone soon, but I need to calm down first," I mumbled.

I imagined lifting the receiver and dialling. Butterflies fluttered recklessly in my stomach, making me nauseous. My thoughts of rejection magnified. I cringed and wondered how my birth mother would react. In my mind she had rejected me once and I feared rejection more than anything. My childhood had been happy and I was married to a kind husband and the mother of three adorable sons. A quote floated through my mind: 'Why reach for the moon when you already have the stars?' I wondered if I should heed the message.

I slumped on the sofa and struggled with my emotions. The parable of Pandora's Box floated into my mind. I remembered it well as my adoptive mother had often recalled it. It felt so relevant at that moment as I wondered, should I use caution and remain safe but ignorant? Or should I open the box as Pandora did?

Although I was a comparatively happy person, I hated being adopted. I had always despised the words adopt, adopted and adopting. On hearing them, I experienced a sharp jab of emotion.

I looked at the phone. Would my birth mother reject me again? Could a mother be so cruel? Maybe I was naïve, romantic or optimistic, but my adoptive parents had given me the gift of feeling special. I was convinced I exuded enough charm to win acceptance. The woman was my birth mother so surely we would weave a relationship.

I wilted in the heat and stared into space. John took my hand and squeezed. I asked him, "What if she rejects me?"

John's clear blue eyes looked into mine with compassion. "It might be better if I phoned. I don't think you should be directly involved. We've no idea how she'll react."

"Are you sure? I feel sick with nerves so I'd be very relieved." I squeezed John's hand and thanked him. The pressure was off as I convinced myself using a third party was the right approach.

"Where's her number?"

I handed John the pad and he lifted the receiver and dialled. I took a deep breath and held my ear to the receiver, listening to the ringtone over the loud thumps of my heart. A minute passed then the phone rang out. What an anti-climax!

"She might be away on holidays," I said, my body surging with adrenalin. "My birth brother might know where she is. We could phone him but we don't have to say who we are."

I discovered his existence in 1981 but did not know his name and I assumed he knew nothing about me.

"Good idea." said John. "If he finds out, it doesn't matter. After all, you're his sister!"

My adoptive parents had presented me with my adoption certificate the previous year. My birth mother's name was Edna Doris McBroom (nee Fechner) and we found her address in the phone directory. She lived only thirty minutes away in Loganlea.

McBroom was an uncommon name, as it had only three listings. The second McBroom lived at West End and the third, a William C. McBroom, lived in Woodridge.

My hands shook as I flicked through the phone book. I scribbled down the number and handed it to John. He dialled and after four rings someone picked up.

"Hello," answered a pleasant female voice.

"Hello. I'm trying to get in touch with Edna McBroom. We thought you might be related."

"Yes, I'm her daughter-in-law. She's away at the moment staying with her friend, Bert, in Rosewood. I'll give you his number."

John took down the number, thanked the woman then hung up the phone. I had assumed correctly. William C. McBroom was my birth brother.

"She sounded nice," said John, "and very friendly."

I thought it odd we did not know her name but I was pleased she sounded agreeable. Maybe I would meet her someday.

"I think we should use Christian names for my birth family otherwise it's too confusing," I suggested.

John agreed so we referred to my birth mother and brother as Edna and Bill.

I said, "I'm not sure we should phone Edna at her friend's place. On the other hand I'm too hyped up to wait."

"I think we should phone her, or something might happen and we'll never do it," said John.

"OK."

John dialled. Eight rings later, someone picked up.

"Sorry to trouble you. Could I speak to Edna McBroom, please?"

"Yeah, just a minute, I'll get her," answered a man in a gruff voice.

As John and I waited for Edna to come to the phone my resolve crumbled. I rejected the drama of the moment and ran into our bedroom, threw myself on the bed and pulled the covers over my head. I curled into a foetal position, clasped my hands over my ears, and squeezed my eyes shut, aghast at what I had done.

As I lay in the dark, wrapped in my misery, my intestines churned and my heart raced. When everything returned to normal and curiosity got the better of me, I eventually poked out my head from under the bedclothes just as John peered around the doorway.

"What happened?" I gasped.

"What happened to you?"

"I had a panic attack. Did you speak to Edna?"

"Yes. After she said hello, I told her my name and explained I was married to her daughter and you'd like to contact her."

"What did she say?"

"She didn't say a thing."

I imagined Edna's shock. No wonder she was speechless.

"Edna didn't speak so I asked 'Could your daughter phone you sometime and have a talk?' and she said, 'I'll be home in two weeks and I'll ring her then' so I gave her our name and number and hung up."

"Did she seem upset?"

"She didn't show any emotion at all."

"What did she sound like?"

"She sounded a bit hard as if she'd had a hard life."

Poor Edna. How did she get through her pregnancy then my relinquishment? I wept. We were mother and daughter but sadly would never know each other as such. For us, time lost could never be regained.

I retired to bed but could not sleep. The sense of loss stayed with me for hours as I contemplated our mutual grief. How had she coped? What pain did she endure? Adoption and loss were natural acquaintances and affected all members of the adoptive triad. I counted out the members of the triad: the adoptive parents, the birthparents and the adoptee. I listed the joys and losses for all of us hoping to help myself fall sleep.

I was still awake after an hour when the story of my friend, Joy, filtered through my mind. Joy, whose father was dead, was seven years old when the authorities removed her from her mother's care. Her mother, who had schizophrenia, was hospitalised unexpectedly. Joy's aunt arrived immediately and snatched her away to avoid the State Children Department. She fought the courts later and was granted custody.

Joy and I have often discussed her loss and my status as an adoptee. On one occasion Joy commented, "You were so lucky, Jean. You had your [adoptive] mother all to yourself. I didn't have that. Aunty May had three daughters and she was good to me, but it wasn't like having my own mother. I really missed having a mother all to myself."

"Yes, I was very lucky to have a lovely relationship with my [adoptive] mother. Joy, I have a question for you."

"OK."

"What would you choose if you had the choice? Would you choose to be adopted with a mother to yourself and never know your biological relatives? Or would you choose to stay in your biological family?"

Joy was silent for a few moments before she replied, "I would choose to stay in my biological family."

Carolann in her adoptive mother's arms in 1948.
Photographer: Jack Gordon.

Carolann in her adoptive parents' garden in 1948.
Photographer: Mary Gordon.

Carolann in 1972 with Chris. Photographer: John Dowding.

2

First Search

Anger simply shows something in you is hurt,
some wound is there.
– Osho

Back in the 1950s I asked my adoptive mother why my birth mother gave me away. I was told that her husband had deserted her. My birth mother worked as the Station Mistress at Ormiston at the time of my birth. Ormiston was one of the many small communities that made up the Redlands. Redland Bay, also part of the same district, was the location of my adoptive parents' home.

In 1981, my concerns with adoption broadened so when I noticed an article in The Courier-Mail, that requested input from anyone affected by adoption, I replied. I commented on the restrictive laws relating to identifying information for adoptees and the frustration I experienced. I mentioned the effects of ignorance of ancestry and medical history. I stressed the importance of answers to the big question, 'Why me?' In due course I received a note thanking me for my input.

Back in the early 1980s John and I began to search for my birth mother. We knew her occupation and residential area so we procured copies of electoral rolls for Ormiston in the late 1940s. We soon realised it was fruitless without her name. I approached my adoptive parents and explained my need to know more. I found it a nerve-wracking task, but fortunately my parents were sympathetic.

My adoptive father produced the adoption documents from his large black safe, an item in our house for as long as I could remember. He also presented me with other related correspondence.

I sat in my parents' living room and my hands shook as I thumbed through the aged papers. My heartbeat was fast and I felt breathless.

My eyes scanned the documents and alighted on my birth name. I sucked in a sharp breath. No way! It couldn't be! But it was Carol Ann. Impossible to believe, but true, John's sister was also named Carol Ann. Even the spelling of our names was identical. Caroline, my mother-in-law, was usually referred to as Carol. John and I were astounded. Funnily enough, Carol was also a name I had especially liked, since 1962, when I met an attractive girl at boarding school with that name.

Then I found Edna. My birth mother's name seemed old fashioned and alien. I searched the document for my birth father. Nothing! How irregular. Everyone assumed it was Edna's husband, but why had she failed to name him? I did not mention the discrepancy to my adoptive parents.

My identity had been changed the moment my adoption was finalised in 1948 and later that year I was christened in St Paul's Anglican Church, Cleveland.

My parents probably hoped I would never search for my birth relatives and who could blame them? But I appreciated their honesty, generosity and obliging attitude. In the past, whenever I had questioned them, they were empathetic although a tad reticent and they never broached the subject of adoption unless I asked. I assumed they had been advised to approach it that way.

A few days after I received the documents my adoptive mother volunteered information. In the 1940s her cousin, June, had lived on a farm behind Edna's cottage. I was intrigued. Had June noticed any family likenesses between Edna and myself?

"Neeny [my nickname], why don't you go and see June? She could probably tell something more about your birth family."

I thanked my mother. I was grateful for her generosity during such a complex situation.

The next day after a quick phone call I set out for Ormiston. June had moved into a new house only a mile or so from the old railway station. She gave me a warm welcome and talked openly about the past. "I remember when Edna arrived in 1947, but I never knew she was pregnant because she was always behind the counter. Doctor Fielding, [the only local doctor], arranged your adoption you know."

I remembered Dr Fielding who had passed away long ago. He had been my doctor in early childhood. How bizarre he had been Edna's doctor too. I wondered if he had delivered me. I thought of all the information that had died with him.

"Your [adoptive] father and [adoptive] grandfather visited Edna. It was a private adoption otherwise that would not occur. Afterwards your grandfather said, 'Why would anyone want to leave a lovely woman like that?'"

I was thrilled to hear the compliment.

"I can't believe Dad actually met her and never mentioned it. Were they checking Edna out?"

"I suppose so," said June. "You know, I helped your Mum and Dad care for you."

"Yes. Mum said you were wonderful support. Thanks for today. I really appreciate it."

"It's my pleasure. You had a [birth] brother you know. He would have been about three when you were born. He was a nice-looking little boy with blond curly hair."

June told me she noticed Edna brought up my birth brother beautifully although she was quite strict and would not stand any nonsense.

"She'd have been a good mother for you," said June. "Mary [my adoptive mother] was too soft with you. Jack [my adoptive father] had to do all the disciplining. You were quite a handful you know."

I could not disagree as my adoptive mother had mentioned I disliked being in my playpen so much I shook it to bits. I loved the way my parents always recounted my pranks in a positive light.

I thought June's comment about Edna and mothering was rather ironic.

"Did you see any other members of Edna's family?"

June mentioned she had seen Edna's three attractive sisters visit at times.

"Did you see any men?"

"No."

"Do you remember what month Edna arrived?"

June could not remember.

"On one occasion Doctor Fielding, Edna and I were in her cottage and you were in her arms. Suddenly she said, 'She's not illegitimate you know'."

"I wonder why she'd say that?" My thoughts whirled. Uncertainties surfaced.

June and I discussed an incident that occurred when my future adoptive parents received a letter from the State Children Department declaring Edna had withdrawn her consent to my adoption and must return me immediately. Needless to say my future adoptive parents were devastated.

State Children Department

William Street, Brisbane

16th February, 1948

Dear Sir,

With reference to your application to adopt the infant Carol Ann McBroom, I wish to inform you that the mother has now written to this department definitely cancelling her consent to the adoption of the child.

Under the circumstances, your application for this child cannot proceed.

However, inquiries will be continued, and, when your application is approved, you will be listed for attention as early as possible.

Yours Faithfully,

S. Brown, Director

"So my Dad took me back to Edna," I said. "Mum said she was too upset to go so Dad drove and you nursed me. Mum told me she was devastated after we'd left. She went a little berserk and dragged my cot down a steep set of steps, threw it under the house, and left for the beach where she walked up and down crying."

"When Jack and I arrived at Edna's cottage he carried you inside," June told me. "I waited in the car for about half an hour and eventually he emerged with you in his arms. I was astounded because Edna had given you back to him. I had never seen anyone as happy as Mary."

"Somehow Dad, who can be very persuasive, must have persuaded Edna to change her mind."

"Your [adoptive] Aunt Jean Jones and her husband Ralph had plenty to say about your adoption. I even heard them ask, 'Where did she come from?' Your Uncle Ralph said, 'She'll never be grateful'."

Uncle Ralph was probably right. I did not ask to be adopted and was always annoyed when someone implied I should be grateful. I admit I have felt subtle pressure to exhibit gratitude. This may happen when an adoptee expresses any negativity about their adoption.

I thanked June and bade her goodbye. I did not go home immediately but deviated to the railway cottage. I parked on the verge and sat for a long time in deep thought.

I had lived here for a very short time. How many times had I driven passed in recent years? I noticed the cottage looked dilapidated now with its cladding of brown stained weatherboards and verandah closed in with glass louvers. The worn galvanised iron roof was faded and a rickety fence surrounded the garden.

I stared at the cottage and tried to envisage being a baby in Edna's womb, behind the counter, in the station. I tried to imagine my life if I had remained in her care. She had cancelled her consent to my adoption when I was one month old, so she must have wanted me. Then I saw her again for about half an hour before I left for my future adoptive home. I wondered how I coped with all the changes. Was I hungry during transportation?

I reflected on the loss of my biological family and it seeped into my soul and psyche. What if another family had adopted me? I sighed. Nothing could change the past.

I was grateful for June's input. I knew nothing about my paternal birth family, but hoped to remedy that someday.

I drove away from the cottage and appreciated the surroundings. The land sloped east towards Moreton Bay where sea views created a splendid panorama. Along the roadsides geometric plots of earth juxtaposed rows of vegetables reminding me that the district was once nicknamed the 'Salad Bowl' for its fruit and vegetable farms. I looked out over the sub-tropical scrub hugging the creeks and across the bay where the sand dunes on Stradbroke Island wore the hazy shades of lavender. The Redlands was my birthplace and I loved it.

Carolann's watercolour, 'Mother and Child', speaks for itself.

Mary and Jack (Carolann's adoptive parents) in 1939.
Unknown Photographer.

Carolann aged sixteen months in 1949. Poulsen Studios.

Edna (Carolann's birth mother) aged thirty-two in 1949.

Cyril (Carolann's birth father) in the 1940s.

Alma Ethel, Cyril's sister (Carolann's birth aunt) in the 1940s. Photographer: family member.

3

The Drive By

The only way to get rid of temptation is to yield to it.
– Oscar Wilde

1982

On the home front, my family life continued smoothly. We made the four-room cottage as comfortable as we could. A sleep-out was added when, in the past, someone had enclosed the narrow front verandah with hopper windows. We partitioned off a miniscule nursery in the sleep-out for Andrew. Chris and Lachlan slept on a double-decker bed at the opposite end. The house rested on low timber stumps with an iron roof and fibro cement cladding.

Sometimes we experienced amusing incidents, such as the night I thought Lachlan had disappeared.

Something woke me so I jumped up and checked on the boys. Seven-year-old Lachlan was missing from his bed. I whispered his name as I searched around the house then returned to his bed and stood thinking. Where could he be?

It was a hot night so all the hopper windows were open. The double-decker bed was pushed against them because the sleep-out was so narrow. I noticed Lachlan's mattress lined up with an open window. Frantically I opened the external door and peered into the garden.

The moon was full and I could see something pale in the shrub under Lachlan's window. I reached into the leaves and my hand touched something soft that turned out to be Lachlan.

I extricated him and was surprised to see he was still asleep. I lifted him up and checked his face and limbs for scratches. He had no apparent injuries probably because he had plunged only a short distance. Implausibly he slept on.

I giggled to myself when I thought of him rolling out the window and landing in the bush without waking. I placed him back in his bed and closed and locked the window. The whole family had a laugh the next day.

My experience of motherhood and incidents like these often reminded me of Edna and all that she had missed. When I lost Lachlan out the window, I wondered if Edna thought of me as she went about her daily tasks of caring for my birth brother Bill in childhood. I reflected often on the pain of giving away a child, and how I did not think I could and was grateful I was never faced with such a decision.

Moments like these compelled me more and more to know Edna and to build something between us to make up for her absence in my childhood.

It was a week since we had first contacted Edna. She was expected home in another week and I hoped she would phone me immediately. I lived in a state of high excitement and fought the impulse to avoid mundane matters like boring household chores such as cleaning and ironing.

I accepted the fact my biological relatives lived only thirty minutes away but were total strangers. I thought about how we could have shopped in the same shopping complex or passed on the street. Their proximity was a weird situation and both tantalised and disturbed me.

I was tempted to do a drive-by of Edna's house but the thought conjured sharp cramps that speared my intestines and I clutched my stomach. I did not wish to hurt my adoptive family and guilt tainted any imaginings of innocent but adoption-related activity.

Still, it was a fine day but I could not settle to any tasks. I longed to drive by Edna's house – just for a look. After breakfast I rushed through the housework, while Chris, Lachlan and Andrew played with Lego.

I searched the garden for John. He was hedging some bushes on the side boundary. I walked purposefully towards him and asked, "Could we do a drive-by of Edna's house today?"

"OK. We'll go after lunch. The kids can come too."

I thanked John and realised his decision to include the children was good. Because of guilt I could not ask my adoptive parents to babysit.

I returned to the cottage and completed more chores. At 11:30am, I assembled the makings of chicken and salad sandwiches. When lunch was ready I called everyone and during the meal explained the drive-by to the children.

"I was adopted, so I have two mothers, Edna and Granny Mary. Edna, who we have never met, gave birth to me and Granny and Grandpa Gordon brought me up."

The boys listened quietly to my explanation, but did not add anything to the conversation. The issue of adoption was a weird topic for my children to understand and at times even I did not want to discuss it. Nevertheless, I tried to be as open and honest as possible. I was grateful that they had trouble understanding it.

After we cleared away lunch, we left the cottage and drove along Gordon Road, entered Queen Street and then turned left into School of Arts Road. We made a hard right turn into Collins Road where we proceeded through miles of tilled farmland. Collins eventually became Serpentine Creek Road and the farms gave way to a forest of stunted eucalypts and acacias.

We followed the road for five minutes before we drove between hills covered with Kikuyu grass. Cows grazed where the remnants of antiquated dairy farms dotted the countryside. Next we crossed Native Dog Creek, wound along acreages that hugged the Logan River and ten miles later met the northbound lane of the Pacific Highway. We blended with the Brisbane traffic for five minutes before we turned left onto the meandering road to Loganlea.

I was thankful I knew Edna was in familiar Rosewood otherwise my nerviness would have been greater. Nevertheless as we drew close to Loganlea the butterflies in my stomach increased dramatically.

John, a whiz with directions, located Edna's house on a

service road that ran parallel to Kingston Road. In the distance I heard the roar of traffic as our car crawled along the deserted street.

Edna's rectangular house was on high posts and looked deserted with every curtain and blind tightly closed. The house was clad with cream chamfer boards and underneath was a built-in garage. A narrow, front verandah had a metal guardrail and a steep set of steps. The garden was neat with a hedge of book leaf pines.

We sat silently in the car. I stared at an ordinary house on an ordinary day but I believed I had achieved something momentous.

"We could go and find Bill's house while we're in the area," suggested John.

"OK, but I don't want him to see us." I was not prepared! I took a Refidex from the glove box and the butterflies in my stomach moved at twice the speed as I flicked through the pages. I passed it to John and he glanced at it quickly.

"It's only a couple of miles up the road," he remarked.

We exited Edna's street and veered north on Kingston Road. Five minutes later we turned left into Bill's Street. John slowed the car and I sunk as low as possible in my seat and peered over the dashboard. As our car crawled along, I scanned the house numbers. Eventually John stopped the car in front of Bill's house. It was bigger than Edna's although of a similar style and well maintained with a neat fenced garden.

Bill's street was a dead end so John drove up and down three times. A man appeared on his front path on the opposite side of the street and glared at us. I decided it was time to leave but I noted the man's eyes followed our car until we disappeared.

"I feel like a criminal."

"You shouldn't," replied John.

We arrived home half an hour later and we went about our business. I contemplated the day and decided I had benefited from viewing Edna and Bill's houses because it took a little courage and it helped me relate to them as 'real' people.

4

Waiting

Waiting, waiting, to belong
in a life I've lived alone.
Cut off, cut out, how cruel
the unknown mother,
with her whips, her tricks, her throwing sticks
and even the cupboard bare of a bone.
– Carolann Carlyle Dowding

1982

Patience is a virtue and very difficult to attain when something exciting is in the offing.

Two weeks passed since the night John contacted Edna and yet, time stood still. I waited for her phone call every day and when it did not come, I suffered the turmoil of deeply conflicting emotions.

By midday, midweek of the third week, I knew Edna would have been home from Rosewood for a number of days. I made a sandwich, took a bite and managed to swallow a tiny mouthful, thinking only of how each day my expectations increased as the hours dragged then disappointment followed. Each time the phone rang, I dropped everything and ran to find out it wasn't her. The order of my day was anticipation versus depression. I longed to have Edna welcome me back into her life. She was 'the mother', but I had made the first move. Now it was her turn.

How would Edna regard my reappearance? I could not begin to imagine. I also knew that Edna could not understand my fear of rejection or how isolation from my biological family had affected me.

I could imagine that life for a relinquishing mother was extremely hard in 1948 when no professional emotional support was available. If my birth were a secret, Edna would have suppressed her pain.

I thought about how people always said birth mothers loved their babies and gave them away to give them the chance of a better life. But still, as far as I was concerned I had been abandoned. I found many adoptive issues confusing but tried to come to terms with it as best I could, especially during this time.

Then, before I knew it four weeks had passed since our phone call to Edna. Was she going to ignore me? It was a painful dilemma.

Every day John arrived home from work to the unexpected. He knew Edna's rejection ate into my heart a little more each day. He would open a bottle of wine and we each enjoyed a glass or two as we discussed her. The stress of the potential reunion with my biological family had already placed quite a strain on me.

5

Scarlet Snow

There are two ways to live your life:
one is as though nothing is a miracle,
the other is as though everything is a miracle.
– Albert Einstein

1982

Although Edna's failure to make contact caused me much anguish, my life at that time was good. Motherhood with three boys had good times and bad, but mostly it was a joyous state for me. Strange to think, as a teenager, I often said I would rather have six Great Danes than have children.

John and I had extended families that helped when tricky situations invariably occurred. My adoptive mother lived down the road and was a wonderful grandmother. My mother-in-law lived twenty minutes away and was also involved in a loving way with her grandchildren.

Chris and Lachlan attended Redland Bay Primary School. Andrew, a toddler, spent his days with me. As a full time wife and mother I had plenty of time alone to churn thoughts of a possible reunion with my birth family.

It was a perfect day. I flung open the cottage door, stepped outside and observed a flawless sky. The temperature was pleasant, a slight breeze ruffled the leaves and in the distance the bay stretched languidly to distant islands. I relaxed as I leant against the doorframe and listened to the birds twitter in the shrubs as an afternoon hush settled over the countryside. I closed my eyes and in the distance I heard the predictable rhythm of a tractor, fast then slow as the machine turned at the furrow's end, a soothing sound from my childhood.

I flapped away a bumblebee and it buzzed across the lawn. Bees hummed in the flowers of the Poinciana tree, and the falling petals covered the earth like scarlet snow.

The natural beauty of my surroundings contrasted with my thoughts as they swung back to a day in 1952 when I learnt everything was not as it seemed; the day I learnt I was adopted.

6

Revelation

For nothing is secret, that shall not be made manifest;
neither anything hid, that shall not be known.
– Luke 18:17

July 1952

I began Prep One, aged four and a half years, at Redland Bay. The timetable was relaxed and included plenty of play and a nap after lunch. The school had the minimum number of pupils required to be a two-teacher school, but the headmaster continually struggled to keep up the numbers. Hence, any child deemed mature enough was encouraged to enroll. I was one of those children.

One afternoon, after school, I leant against the kitchen table and watched as my mother deftly rolled out pastry on a marble slab. We discussed our day and then the subject changed and included the word adoption. Our conversation dissolved with time, but I remember she explained I was her adopted daughter. Someone else, not she, had given birth to me.

I was astounded and in my mind, my status in the family plummeted. My childhood brain whirled. One minute I belonged completely to my family then a minute later I did not. If only I could return to the safe fuzzy moment before my mother said 'You are adopted'.

My mother spoke gently and encouraged me to accept this news about my adoption. She said, "We chose you, so you're very special. Dad wasn't a natural baby lover like I was. I loved every baby I saw but when Dad saw you he knew you were the one."

Despite her efforts, I was suspicious about the 'chosen' story. It did not make up for the shocking revelation. I thought the word 'adopted' was repulsive.

After the adoption revelation, my adoptive mother returned to her cooking. She acted as if nothing out of the ordinary had happened and no one mentioned adoption again. I moved into a silent world as far as adoption was concerned and pretended everything was fine. I ate dinner that night in a safe, warm environment, carefree, except for what I felt was my new adoptive status. My mother served a delicious meal and almost everything was back to normal, but I had a feeling life would never be exactly the same.

And it never was.

I learnt the truth on an ordinary day that ended as extraordinary. Later, I learnt being told about my adoption was, according to researchers, my 'second trauma', with the first the separation from my birth mother. Unfortunately counselling for members of the adoption triad was unheard of in the 1940s and 1950s. Today awareness of adoption is much greater and counselling is widely available and adoptees are free to speak about their experiences.

From the day of revelation I have contended with my adoption. Even today, at sixty-four, I still grapple with issues, despite the fact that I was extremely lucky to be adopted by a good family.

Life with my adoptive parents was pleasant and stable. My days revolved around home, farm, garden, beach, boats and school.

Fresh fruit and vegetables were plentiful and thrived on our farm. Fruit, such as citrus and stone, that did not prosper was bought from the Rocklea markets in Brisbane. My father and his brother, Uncle Bobby and his wife, Aunt Daphne, our next door neighbours, collected their orders when they delivered their produce.

My father joined local residents to fish, hunt wild ducks and hook mud crabs along the shores of Moreton Bay and the banks of the Logan River. Consequently we enjoyed many interesting foods, including roast wild duck, natural oysters and other seafood. I remember my mother roasting a rabbit gifted by a local hunter. Eggs were plentiful. The hens lived in a pen in the paddock that ran between our house and my Uncle Bobby's and Aunt Daphne's. In the early 1950s we shared a cow and my adoptive father and uncle took turns milking it.

Once, Ian and I were delighted when someone gave us a wallaby. We tried to tame it but one day it jumped over the verandah rail, landed in the garden six foot below, and hopped away unharmed.

Biddy, a black curly coat retriever, gave birth to many litters of puppies much to our delight. When Biddy came in season every six months, my father locked her in the backyard laundry. One morning he pulled open the door and Biddy emerged with her 'boyfriend' who had apparently scraped open a window during the night. Sure enough, eight weeks later, another twelve puppies emerged and I was allowed to keep one.

A few days after heavy rain, my adoptive mother and I loved to walk down the road to a paddock where mushrooms flourished. She taught me to recognise edible fungi and later cooked up a nice feast.

My adoptive parents owned Tilba, a nine metre bay cruiser. She was moored in the bay directly in front of our house. On our yearly summer holidays we lived on board for two or three weeks.

My father would anchor at Jumpinpin on South Stradbroke Island, or the Southport Basin. Ian and I had great fun sliding down the steep sand hills. I collected shells and if it rained we played board games.

Tilba was not equipped with a shower so after dark, when Ian and I were very young, we stood naked on the duckboard, while one of our parents poured buckets of water over us. At night everyone slept soundly lulled by the lap of waves on the hull.

I loved our home with its hat shaped galvanised iron roof, painted a cheerful red, and wide verandahs accessed from French doors and huge push up windows. Inside, pressed metal ceilings embossed with attractive symmetrical patterns were featured in many of the rooms.

My adoptive mother, a skilled homemaker and gardener, placed fresh flowers in the rooms to accentuate the ambience. The house stood near the edge of red cliffs, sparsely covered with the dark trunks of iron bark trees, and Bribie Island pines, through which we had a view across Moreton Bay.

Carolann's childhood home in Redland Bay.
Photographer: C. Dowding.

7

The Reluctant Birth Mother

What lies behind us,
and what lies before us,
are tiny matters,
to what lies within us.
– Oliver Wendell Homes

1982

The sun shone brightly and created a swathe of sparkles across the bay. I sat on the top step and pondered adoption and the many challenges it presented. Despite the magnificent day my equilibrium was threatened. Edna had still not contacted me.

Would I suffer rejection again at the hands of my birth mother? I knew my adoptive parents wanted me, but that did not take the place of finding love and acceptance from the woman who brought me into the world.

I seemed challenged to face my fears and take action, even while I fretted about the outcome. The preceding weeks had tested my endurance and my feelings of helplessness had multiplied.

I sat on the steps and contemplated my dilemma then made a decision that would move me towards my destiny.

I strolled into the cottage and stared at the phone. I was alone except for Andrew who was sound asleep in the nursery. I clenched my jaws while the muscles in the back of my neck tightened into a vice-like grip.

I entered the kitchen and searched in the cupboards. At last I found a bottle of Woodley's Three Roses Sherry, a gift from my adoptive father, the only alcohol in the house. I poured out a generous measure, returned to the living room, and balanced on the edge of the couch.

I sipped the liquid and it burnt a path down my throat followed by a fiery sensation that licked at the lining of my stomach. Fifteen minutes later I had relaxed a little but my heart still hammered as I ambled to the phone. My hands shook as I lifted the receiver and dialled. I counted six rings. The ring tone seemed excruciatingly loud and I almost slammed the receiver down before someone picked up.

"Hello," said a brusque female voice.

"He-hello is that Edna McBroom?"

"Yes," she answered.

"I'm. I'm your daughter, Jean," I blurted. "You, you know wh-who I mean?"

"Oh you know your husband nearly gave me a heart attack ringing me that night," she said.

I scanned my mind for something to say but she continued.

"I've already suffered two heart attacks, one major when I was only fifty-eight," she snapped.

I was staggered. I could not believe Edna's first words to me were in the form of a reprimand. She was definitely peeved and did not display the same characteristics as my gentle adoptive mother who always treated me with kindness, love and respect.

In recent weeks I had been under such great strain, I found the tension too much and tears welled up in my eyes and ran down my cheeks.

"When your husband rang I was so shocked. I'm not well you know. I was in hospital for three months and almost died then I contracted golden staph and I've never been the same since. I suffer from dizziness and nausea continually. It's something to do with my balance."

"I'm s-s-sorry," my voice broke on a sob.

"Oh, don't cry, love," said Edna. "It's just that I don't want another heart attack."

I wiped my eyes. Edna had recounted her suffering with a skill that extracted sympathy and she took a superior stance from the first moment of our relationship.

"I'm sorry," I said. "We had no idea." Then I wondered how I would address Edna and asked, "What will I call you, er, Mum?"

"Oh, no. No. Edna will do. Anyway how on earth did you find me?" she asked.

"Dad gave me my adoption papers."

"Why on earth would he do that?"

"Because I asked him to," I said.

I noted Edna's incredulous tone and her horror that such an event could take place.

"Why did they tell you that you were adopted?" she said. "That's cruel! I thought you'd never find out,"

"They were told it was the right thing to do," I answered. "They believed I had a right to know."

Edna's negativity inflamed me. She had criticised my adoptive parents and I felt challenged to defend them. Children's Services had advised them to be truthful to an adoptee and they had always believed 'honesty is the best policy'. I decided Edna must be ignorant of correct adoption procedures.

I felt that Edna and I were on a collision course with the conversation so I changed the topic.

"Were you deserted by your husband?"

"Yes."

"Is that why I was given up?" I asked.

"Yes. I wanted to keep you, but I didn't have any money and nor did my family. I already had one child and had to work full time. I couldn't look after both of you."

Edna explained that she could not go home to her mother because her stepfather and one of her half-brothers were chronic alcoholics.

I empathised with her and said I understood.

"We didn't have an easy life," she told me. "In 1925, when I was seven years old my father, who was only forty, died of a cerebral haemorrhage. I had four brothers and sisters, the youngest no more than two months old. We were almost destitute."

I was interested in Edna's tragedy. In a sense it was mine too, but I suspected she used it to justify my adoption.

"My father worked for Queensland Railways before his death, so they offered my mother a job as gatekeeper at Walloon. A free house was included so we survived."

I learnt Walloon was near Rosewood just off the Toowoomba Highway. A few years after her father's death, Edna's mother remarried and gave birth to three more children.

"Phew!" I said. "Eight children was such a large family."

"Yes, it was," said Edna. "We were older though, so we helped Mum with the babies and the gates,"

Edna explained that when she was twelve years old she took a test conducted by the Education Department to ascertain her level of competence. She passed with flying colours and was permitted to leave school and assist her mother with home duties.

"Mum retired in 1952 but she had to move out of the railway house. My stepfather drank heavily and wasted money on alcohol and we hated him. Eventually Mum could not stand his and her youngest son's heavy drinking so she left them and moved to Leichardt to live with Ben, her third youngest child. At times she returned to Walloon to clean up the house, but gave that up eventually."

I empathised with Edna about the hard times her family had experienced. Then I asked a very important question. "Did you ever think about me?"

"Yes, of course I did," said Edna. "When you were born you were the spitting image of me. Giving you away was like cutting off my right arm."

"Did anyone else know you'd had me?"

"My mother." said Edna. "She said I couldn't do it, but in the end there was no choice. I just couldn't keep you. You know, it's strange, but all I ever wanted was a family of my own."

"Is your mother still alive?"

"No. She died of bowel cancer in 1975, aged eighty–six."

"That's sad, but she had a long life."

I asked Edna if she remembered June, who had lived near her in the 1940s. I explained that she was my adoptive mother's cousin. Edna remembered her. Then I asked, "I've always loved art and spend lots of time drawing. Was anyone in the family into art?"

"Yes," she said, "Me. I started to draw when I was about four years old."

Edna explained how she would sit by herself and draw flowers. When she was older she loved to draw old houses. She said if she had had more time, she would have loved to develop her drawing.

"I started drawing about the same age." I asked, "Were any of our ancestors artists?"

"Yes, a long way back in Germany."

I was thrilled I had found a link to my ancestors, an artistic trait handed down through the generations. I told her, "In the 1960s I was granted a scholarship to Art College, based on my junior results. I studied there for four years doing a Diploma in Commercial Illustration."

Edna and I knew so little about each other, I was delighted we were sharing a little of our past.

"What nationality is your maiden name, Fechner?" I asked.

"German," she said. "My mother's maiden name was, Siemsen, also German. Other names in the family are Kruger, Kowalski and Karrasch."

Edna's mother and father, although of Western European origin, had been born in Brisbane in 1889 and 1884 respectively.

I mentioned my sons, Chris, Lachlan and Andrew and my membership in the Nursing Mothers Association. I said I was proud I had successfully breastfed my babies.

"The hospital staff made me breastfeed you," said Edna bluntly. Her statement left me speechless. She had been obligated to feed me, nothing more, while I had been so loving and conscientious towards my babies.

During our conversation, I felt torn. Edna did not seem to have much sensitivity, or was I too easily hurt. I attempted to put her attitude in perspective and decided she was not adept at putting herself in another's shoes.

"I could have had an abortion you know," Edna told me.

What a terrible thing to say; stupid and cruel. My mouth dried out and her statement brought me face to face with my mortality. 'Death on a whim while still in the womb'. How horrendous.

Now was the moment I should thank Edna for sparing my life, but something prevented me. Why did she carry me to full term? I could not bring myself to ask. Our conversation was on a collision course again so I changed the topic.

"I'd like to come to see you," I said.

"No," said Edna. "No. I don't think that would be a good idea."

I was taken aback. "Why not? I'd like to be a daughter to you."

Edna explained she was not well enough to cope with me in her life partly because of the dizziness and nausea. If I had found her ten years earlier things might have been different. She had never told anyone about me and could not face all the drama.

I was baffled. How could a mother not wish to meet her daughter? Edna's refusal to meet me hit me hard. It was the second rejection I had been dreading. I was devastated.

"I've retired after working all my life and I want to relax and enjoy it," she told me. "If Tevy [my birth brother, Bill] knew what I'd done he wouldn't love me anymore. He's all I've got, and I couldn't bear to lose him. You're OK. You've got so much more,"

How could Edna know what I did or did not have?

"Couldn't we just tell Bill?" I persisted.

"No. His marriage isn't very stable so this might push it over the edge. It's definitely not the right time to tell him."

Edna was unyielding. She seemed to have no understanding of adoptive issues, assumed I did not need her and was uncaring about our biological bond. And she still feared being rejected by her family.

I did not know what to say next so I asked an unrelated question.

"What work does Bill do?"

"He's a cabinetmaker at Stegbar."

I heard Andrew start to coo in his cot so I kept my ear on him as Edna and I continued our conversation. Five minutes later Andrew started to cry.

"Andy's crying. I'll just go and get him."

"Yes, go to the little one," said Edna.

I arrived back a few moments later with Andrew nestled on my hip.

"I'd like to phone you again if that's OK. When would be a good time?" I asked.

"Well," she said. "Tuesday morning would safe. I'm always alone then."

Edna and I said good-bye and hung up. I walked aimlessly around the house with Andrew on my hip. She did not want to meet me and it felt like a rejection.

I tried to comfort myself. At least we would have secret phone calls. How ironic, I thought at the time. Our new relationship will start with secrecy, one of the prime foundations of adoption.

After we talked that first time, I realised there was so much I wanted to tell her. In future conversations with Edna I hoped to share so much with her, to help her understand who I was, who I had become in her absence.

I wanted to tell her that in 1967, during the college holidays, Myers Department Store employed me as a layout, paste up and photo retouch artist. I worked in the roof top studio, in the old McWhiter building in Fortitude Valley. My work was featured in advertisements in *The Courier-Mail* and *The Telegraph*. I wanted her to know that in October 1968 I left art college and began work with commercial artists, David Atkinson and Associates in Fortitude Valley.

I wanted to tell her that on the 3rd of May 1969 John and I were married in St Paul's Anglican Church in Cleveland. Our honeymoon was a weeklong car trip to Sydney when we alternated between camping out in our two-man tent and staying in motels. At the end of the week we returned to Warwick to start our married life where John taught Agricultural Science at the local high school.

I wanted to tell her about my sons and share the funny incidents that had happened to me as the mother of three boys. I longed to tell her about my pregnancies, a subject that mothers and daughters usually shared.

I carried Andrew out into the garden in front of the cottage and put him down. He toddled about on the grass and tried to pat Snoopy, our basset hound. I gazed towards the bay and contemplated my next contact with Edna.

Edna (Carolann's birth mother) with her grandson Alex in 1974.
Photographer: family member.

8

Fantasies, Fears, Dreams and Other Experiences

In the dim dream the shadows were immense
they covered his face, his torso, his legs, arms;
– Shelton Lea, from '*My Unknown Father*' from Nebuchadnezzar

1950s

As a child I fantasised about my birth family but it was not one of the popular adoptee fantasies like, 'my birth mother is a princess who will someday come to claim me'.

I also fantasised I was biologically related to my adoptive family because I longed to find a biological connection; I loved my adoptive family; and my adoptive family were my only reality.

I used to entertain the following fantasies:

1. My adoptive father had an affair with my birth mother.
2. An adoptive uncle had an affair with my birth mother.
3. My adoptive grandfather had an affair with my birth mother.
4. My adoptive father paid my birth mother to be a surrogate mother.

I would have felt more secure if I had been biologically connected to my adoptive family somehow and would have no need to search. And at least I would have known half my genetics.

My mind often whirled with crazy possibilities and I lived in a private world where the figments of my imagination could be as strange as I wished. My first 'truth' had been shattered when I learnt I was adopted. After that, I lived under the shadow of negative expectations.

I succumbed to fears during my childhood and particularly remember once, waking in the middle of the night and peering into the blackness. I had always been afraid of the dark, but I was more petrified than usual. The silence was foreboding so I forced my eyes wide open and tried not to blink. Pale forms floated into focus.

I clenched my hands and wriggled to the centre of the bed. My eyeballs shifted to and fro as I obsessed over each spook-like shape. Finally, after my eyesight had adjusted, the forms materialised into familiar objects that had always been part of my bedroom. Relief flooded through me.

I expelled the breath I had been holding, propped myself up on one elbow and leaned in the direction of my bedroom door. It was open and my eyes strained through the dark to the hall beyond.

I thought longingly of my adoptive parents' bedroom. The only sound was the grandmother clock as it ticked loudly in the next room.

I continued to stare through the dark then froze when a pale wobbly apparition materialised.

Please let it be my mother in her dressing gown.

"Mum?" I croaked.

No answer. I was transfixed. My heart pounded as the hazy form swished closer and halted just inside my doorway. Then incredibly, the face of a young man transpired out of nowhere. He had a benign expression, lightly tanned skin and dark brown curly hair. He appeared clad in a long garment.

"Mum," I croaked. Fear had dried my mouth and I had no volume. "Mum!" I shrieked and shattered the silence.

The apparition swirled around and floated up the hall out of sight. My heart thudded wildly and I longed for my mother but I had to cross the menacing hallway. I summoned every bit of courage I possessed, leapt from my bed and bounded across. Once I was safe I clawed my way into bed beside my mother. And there I stayed for the remainder of the night.

My parents questioned me the next morning. I said something had scared me. I omitted to mention the apparition with the face. Would anyone have believed me?

During my childhood after discovering my adoption, I also succumbed to vivid dreams.

Once I dreamt I was standing alone in an endless flat landscape where the earth was cracked into billions of crazy paving-shaped pieces. The ugly scene seriously disturbed me and I felt compelled to remove every piece.

I forced my fingers into the cracks and started to pry up the pieces. I worked fast and my fingers pained with the effort and my stomach cramped with frustration. How would I complete such a task? Nausea accompanied the sensation. Fortunately I woke up and was relieved to find it was only a dream.

When I got older, I wondered about the nauseating level of frustration I experienced as I tried to remove all the pieces of cracked earth. I wondered if I was striving for something unattainable and if adoptive issues were involved.

Not long after my adoption revelation I thought of a startling question. It was one only my adoptive mother could answer.

I ran through the house and eventually found her in a bedroom changing the sheets. She looked at me and smiled a crooked smile as she held a pillow under her chin and manipulated a clean slip into place. I stood in the doorway and panted.

"Is something wrong, Neeny?" asked my mother.

"Is Ian adopted too?"

"No, dear, he's not."

"Why not?"

"Well it's a long story. Dad and I tried to have a baby for nine years before we adopted you."

I concentrated on my mother's explanation. I loved to hear tales of the past, especially if they included me. With luck I might find out more about my adoption.

"Dad was thirty-four and I was thirty-five when you came into our lives. Of course we were no longer desperate and when you were almost three we considered adopting another girl. We were on the verge of making the first inquiry when I discovered I was going to have a baby."

"Was that baby Ian?"

"Yes. I was thirty-nine when he was born. Before we adopted you we looked after another baby, a little boy, who we hoped to adopt."

"What happened to him?"

"Well I'd made an appointment with the doctor so I took the baby with me. Doctor Fielding asked how we were getting on. I said everything was fine for me, but Dad just couldn't seem to take to the baby."

My mother put her arm around my shoulders and continued her story. "The doctor decided to examine the baby. He undressed him and checked him over carefully. After a few moments he looked up thoughtfully and said, 'This baby's got black blood in him'. Apparently he could tell from the colour of the baby's private parts."

"What happened next?"

"Well, when I arrived home, I told Dad. He immediately contacted the State Children Department and asked that our application to adopt the boy be cancelled. He said he hadn't asked for a mixed race baby. I was very distressed, but there was no option, I had to give him back."

Not for a minute did I think my adoptive parents would send me back. I was secure in their love, but I felt sad for the baby boy who was returned to the department. I hoped he found a loving family. If my parents had adopted him they may not have adopted me. Where would I be now? Or should I say, who would I be now?

I continued to ask my mother questions. "Are any of my ten cousins adopted?"

"No."

Drat! I hated being the odd one out. Ian was my parents 'real' child so I imagined I would always be at a disadvantage. How could I compete with a 'real' child? If Ian had been an adoptee, I would not have been the odd one out.

She told me I was happy being my adoptive parents' only child for three years and eight months before Ian was born. After his birth, I remembered that I had to share everything and I did not like it. I experienced some resentment towards him that continued when he was a toddler.

When Ian and I were older however, jealousy was not a problem. We were opposite sexes with diverse interests and different friends. We very seldom fought although I remember four incidents.

One such incident occurred one night after dinner. As usual, my adoptive father called out to me, "Jean, help Mum wash up."

I had noticed Ian was never asked to help so on this occasion I demanded he help me dry the dishes. He refused so I grabbed a broom and started to chase him through the house. We eventually ran down the road and completely around the whole block dressed in our pyjamas. We thought we were hilarious but our dear mother had finished the dishes when we returned.

I must admit, at times, I imagined my adoptive parents cared more for Ian because he was their biological child. I will never know the answer, but I sometimes wondered if Ian and I were drowning, whom would my father save if he could save only one of us?

Adoptees and birth parents are not the only members of the adoption triad to experience rejection. My adoptive mother confided that she experienced it in the 1940s for her failure to produce offspring. Her mother-in-law, who visited frequently, would often ask, "No babies yet, Mary?"

My mother wished to fall pregnant more than anything else in the world, so the constant reminder of her failure was exceedingly hurtful. She said she was mortified people might think she was 'doing something' to prevent pregnancy.

'The Dream' is based on one of Carolann's childhood dreams.
Photographer: C. Dowding.

9

More Revelations

Tell me the tales that to me were so dear,
Long long ago, long, long ago.
– Thomas Haynes Bayly

1982

Tuesday dawned and I phoned Edna. She answered in a forthright manner and we chatted about nothing in particular until I plucked up the courage to ask some personal questions. "Was your husband my birth father?"

"No," explained Edna, "I married an American serviceman, Edwin McBroom, in 1942, but we were together for only a short time before he was sent back to the war. I was pregnant and had a miscarriage half way through. It was a girl."

"That's sad. Miscarriages are very upsetting. I've had two."

"After I lost the baby, I was discharged from hospital and went straight back to work. A few days later I fell ill. My doctor hospitalised me with severe septicaemia and I almost died.

"My husband, who was on leave, did not bother to inform my family so they found out purely by chance. I wasn't very happy with him. He was recalled to the war soon after and never returned. In 1944 I became involved with another American."

"Was he my birth father?"

"Yes," said Edna. [I would find out later I needed to be wary of how truthful Edna was.]

"Is he Bill's father too?"

"Yes."

I was excited to hear Bill and I had the same birth father! "What happened to him?"

"He went back to America to see his parents after the war but we wrote to each other regularly. Suddenly the letters stopped coming. Some time later I received a letter from his parents that informed me he'd died of a cerebral haemorrhage while working on the railway lines. And they blamed me for his death."

"That's unbelievable," I said. "Why would they do that?"

"I don't know," said Edna. "His parents said he'd worked too hard in the heat to earn money to get back to me. They believed he would never have taken that job if it weren't for me and they were also sorry he'd ever met me."

"You must've been so upset."

"I was. I was so angry, I burnt all his letters."

"What was his name?" I asked.

"Winston Carl Tevis. That's why your brother's nickname is 'Tevy'. He was from Indiana."

"How old was he when he died?"

"Thirty-seven."

"Would you have a photo you could send me?"

Edna explained she did not have any 'snaps' left as she had burnt them too. She said she might have one tiny one left, but she would want it returned. I thanked her and asked if she would send some photos of herself.

"All right, but I don't have many and I want them back," she reminded me.

I reassured her I would return her photos. Then I racked my brain for more questions while Edna was in a talkative mood. "I'm confused about my birthplace. On one document it's Cleveland and on another it's Brisbane."

"I almost died when you were born," said Edna. "During your birth we were transferred from the Cleveland Hospital to the Royal Women's in Brisbane."

I was too reticent to ask Edna why she had almost died. It seemed like another reason to be unwanted. Perhaps it was better not to know.

Edna elaborated on her family. Her older sister and brother-in-law, Margaret and Phil McCloud, had adopted a baby girl. The baby's birth mother was Fran, Margaret and Edna's younger sister. Fran, already a single mother, was not able to care for two young children.

"What was the baby's name?"

"Susan," Edna said. "She's about six months older than you. Susan was never told she was adopted although everyone else in the family knew. Her birth family and adoptive family always avoided going to the same family gatherings as they feared the truth might come out."

I was astonished I had a birth cousin who was also an adoptee but unlike me she had stayed in her biological family.

My thoughts returned to Edna and our discussion. "Do you still see your family?"

"Yes. I'm very close to Susan especially since her mother died. She visits me quite often and I talk to my sister Fran on the phone almost every day."

I prickled with annoyance. A little green monster stabbed my heart and feelings of isolation followed. I felt indignant because Edna had kept me out of her life, but was close to her sister and niece. I managed to keep a lid on my feelings, ashamed of my reaction. "How long ago did your sister, Margaret, die?"

"Seven years. She was only sixty-three, but she was overweight with numerous health problems. She had high blood pressure, Type Two Diabetes and was also a smoker. Unfortunately, her health problems multiplied when something awful happened."

"What was that?

"When Susan was in her teens one of her cousins told her she was adopted. Margaret was never the same after that. When Susan found out the truth, it killed my sister."

Phew! Some of my birth relatives disliked facing the truth. Edna's response was certainly negative. I wondered if it meant a warning to me. Was Edna trying to manipulate me somehow?

10

American Connections

Happiness resides not in possessions
and not in gold
the feeling of happiness dwells
in the soul.
– Democritus

1982

I was disappointed my birth father was dead, although, I now had enough information to search for my paternal birth family. I shared my latest exciting news with John.

Later that week we visited the local post office and looked up my birth father's surname in the overseas phone directory. I made quite an extensive list of Indiana residents.

During the next week I organised photos of my family and myself and wrote relevant messages. I included a duplicate of myself that Edna might like to keep and posted them to her with a hopeful heart.

Tuesday I phoned Edna. She did not mention the photos so I presumed they were still in the post.

"Where did you live before Loganlea?" I asked.

"Taringa. We were there from 1961 to 1978. I was promoted to a first class station mistress," Edna said proudly. "And I loved the spacious railway house we lived in. It was a typical Queenslander."

Edna discussed her first heart attack, in 1975, shortly after her mother's death. She thought stress, while nursing her mother followed by her death were contributing factors.

"Bert, an old beau from my teenage years, and I had just started to date," said Edna. "Then came the heart attack and three months in hospital. When I recovered I returned to work for a while then retired in 1978. Of course I had to move out of the railway house so Bert contributed half the money for this house."

"Does Bert live with you?"

"No. He lives in Rosewood," replied Edna.

"Where did you live before Taringa?"

"Oxford Park," explained Edna. "Although in the late 40s and early 50s we were five years at Ormiston. After that we lived at Lawnton then Calvert. And we were at Thorneside for a short time in the late 1950s."

I was startled that Edna and Tev had lived in such close proximity to my childhood home. We could have attended the same yearly inter-school sports day. I returned to my conversation with Edna.

"Does Bill have any children?"

"Yes, a son named Alexander who is eight years old."

Edna explained that after Alex's birth, his mother Marnie was diagnosed with rheumatoid arthritis and unable to care for him.

Edna applied for long service leave and took over Alex's care. How ironic. She relinquished me in 1948 because she had to work. In 1974 she was able to take leave to care for her grandson.

Edna said goodbye and we parted on good terms.

The following Tuesday I phoned Edna again but she was agitated because the parcel of photos I had sent was left by mistake near a neighbour's letterbox. The neighbour returned it just as Edna's family arrived.

"I was so frightened they'd see your name and ask me about you," said Edna.

"I didn't mention anything to you because I wanted it to be a surprise. Did you enjoy the photos? Do I look like anyone in the family?"

"No," said Edna. "Although when you were born you were the spitting image of me."

I was quite disappointed Edna said I did not resemble anyone. After a few more minutes of conversation I noticed she seemed discomforted and I assumed it was more than the lost parcel.

"Were you upset when you saw my photos?" I asked.

"Yes, I was," answered Edna.

"Because you saw my life?"

"Yes."

I was disillusioned. I thought it was imperative that Edna familiarise herself with my life, otherwise how could our relationship grow? But why did she seem so resistant?

According to June, my first contact in my search, there was an occasion in the 1950s when Edna and I ended up in the same place at the same time.

June was at the Cleveland Show with her family when she saw Edna and Tev. I was there too, with my adoptive parents. They had put me on the merry go round behind June's daughter, Marylou. June said Edna knew Marylou, guessed who I was, and just stared at me.

Years later, my adoptive Aunt Daphne, who lived next door to my adoptive parents, said she saw a woman she thought was my birth mother in the doctor's surgery in the 1950s. Apparently our likeness had clued her up.

Human beings like to see themselves reflected in their relatives' features and mannerisms. Researchers call it 'mirroring'.

Mirroring was not part of my life until I had my own children. I was a bit obsessed about it and was upset if anyone suggested my children were more like someone else. It is acknowledged that a huge percentage of adoptees wish to find their birth families and someone they resemble.

Susan, my birth cousin, did have the opportunity to mirror her birth relatives because she was adopted within her biological family. Her adoptive mother, Margaret, was her biological aunt and her Aunt Fran was her birth mother.

Most adoptees are not as fortunate as Susan and miss out on the advantages of mirroring. Researchers have suggested that mirroring gives more meaning to our lives, enhances our relationships and develops self-esteem. In short, we can see that we fit in to a group and that the group fits in with us.

Over time, I saw that people were often surprised when they found out I was adopted. Some said they thought I looked like my adoptive mother. It was advantageous my adoptive mother and I were the same height with brown hair and similar coloured eyes. When people suggested we were alike, I suffered from both a sweet and a sour reaction, because I knew it could not be true.

Collette Glazebrook featured an interesting analogy in her book, *Facing the Fears*. She used an excerpt from The Bunyip of Berkeley's Creek to illustrate the passion of many adoptees to find someone who resembles them.

> Late one night, a bunyip comes out of the murky mud in the billabong at the bottom of Berkley's Creek. 'What am I,' it asks the various animals of the forest. 'What do I look like?' Of course, many simply run or swim away in fright. Others tell him the truth as they see it: he is a bunyip, and bunyips are horrible, ugly creatures. He meets a scientist, who, without even bothering to look up from his notebook and pencil tells him emphatically that bunyips do not exist. Finally, he dejectedly wanders off until he finds another billabong and sits down beside it.
>
> Something stirs in the murky depths, and out comes something large and muddy. 'What am I?' 'What do I look like?' it asks. The bunyip is ecstatic. 'You look just like me,' he shouts. And he lent her his mirror to prove it.

One Saturday, John and I prepared for our first phone call to my birth father's family in America. Making an overseas phone call was a rarity and John and I struggled to work out the time difference. Eventually we solved the problem so John picked up the receiver and dialled. I was quite calm and stood close. I listened as the phone rang ten times. At last someone picked up.

"Hello," groaned a very sleepy male voice.

"Gee, sorry, mate,' said John. "Did I get you out of bed? I'm calling from Australia."

"No kidding! It's 3.00a.m. here," yawned the sleepy man.

"I'm really sorry, mate," said John. "But I'm looking for relatives of a man named Winston Carl Tevis."

"Sorry I can't help you, buddy."

"That's OK. Thanks for your help, and sorry I woke you."

Later in the week I randomly chose another number for a Tevis and phoned America. The phone rang and rang. Finally someone picked up.

"Hel-lo," slurred a male voice.

"Hello. I'm calling from Australia," I explained. "I'm trying to locate the relatives of a man named Winston Carl Tevis."

"Shsnever snerd of him," the man said.

"Oh. Thanks anyway. Sorry to trouble you." I hung up the phone and giggled. The man sounded seriously intoxicated.

I had not found anything specific regarding my paternal birth family but at least I had begun to search. I had read that an adoptee may suffer from a sense of helplessness and powerlessness and felt that I was no exception. Being in control of my own searches started to reclaim some of that lost power.

John and I discussed the next step in my search and determined it would be too expensive to call every Tevis in Indiana. We put the family history aside for the time being and concentrated on our home life.

Edna (Carolann's birth mother), in the centre, with her son, Tev, and grandson, Alex, in the 1980s. Photographer: family member.

11

Adoption Experiences

To cultivate kindness
is an important part
of the business of life.
– Samuel Johnson

Adoptees usually develop into one of two types, compliant adoptees and acting out, rebellious adoptees.

I am a compliant adoptee. Or at least I learnt to be after attracting trouble at home as a toddler and in early childhood. A compliant adoptee aims to fit in with family, cause no waves, and, above all else, wishes to be loved and accepted.

When I was older I understood that I was expected to fit into my adoptive family and I tried hard to achieve that, but I still had my struggles.

I remember that my father smacked me occasionally. I also remember my adoptive aunt, Daphne, telling her daughter Pam, 'I always felt sorry for Jean as I thought Jack [my adoptive father] was too hard on her.'

My adoptive father was the disciplinarian in the family but my brother, Ian, did not seem to attract the trouble I did. He was my adoptive parents' biological child and I figured that he probably fitted into the family much better than I did.

Years later Ian told me his thoughts on the matter. On one occasion when he was in trouble he thought, 'Now I'm in trouble too. Surely Jean will love me.'

I was happy to have cousins, Bobby and Daphne's children, live next door in early childhood. My adoptive cousin, Donny was one year older than I was and we enjoyed playing together until he started school, and even getting into some mischief.

As pre-schoolers, Donny and I were responsible for the demise of my adoptive father's 1903 Renault that had been fashioned into a utility during the war.

One day, after eating some pollard (powdered horse feed) from the shed, Donny and I decided it would be fun to fill the radiator of the Renault with it. We were busy little bees and spent ages pouring the pollard right into the radiator.

Donny and I were caught eventually but not punished, since the vehicle was not used anymore.

It was not long after the pollard incident that Donny started school. So in January 1952 I sat on the front steps of my house, looking quite dejected. My adoptive mother asked if something was wrong.

"Donny's gone to school so I've no one to play with."

Five months later my adoptive parents enrolled me into Prep One.

My Prep One teacher, Mrs Barnes, was an agreeable, kind and enthusiastic person who made each day pleasurable.

Although I was very young I adapted well to my new experiences and made friends easily. One of those friends, DiAnne, became a lifelong friend.

Redland Bay Primary was a small school with a mere 150 pupils so we all knew each other. My school life progressed smoothly and was stable except for one adoption related incident in 1959. A new pupil walked up to me in the playground.

"You're adopted, aren't you?" she said in a snide manner.

"Yes," I answered truthfully. What a snoop, I thought, wary of ridicule on her part.

"Who told you?" I asked.

"Pam."

I walked off in disgust. Pam – my adoptive cousin, my next-door neighbour, my good friend. I felt betrayed and fumed all day. After school my adoptive mother noticed my mood and questioned me. I explained about Pam and the nosy girl. I finished with a tough statement. "And I'm never going to speak to Pam again!"

"Never mind, dear, everything will be alright. I'll go and see Pam and explain how upset you are."

My mother departed. I was not embarrassed to have caused a fuss. I felt entitled. Half an hour later my mother returned. Pam trailed behind her.

"Pam's come to say sorry, then you'll be friends again, OK?" said my mother.

"Sorry, Jean. I'll never tell anyone else," mumbled Pam.

"That's OK," I said gruffly.

I was vindicated because my mother and Pam were sensitive to my feelings and our friendship resumed immediately. She had only spoken the truth, unfortunately to a troublemaker. No one mentioned the incident again.

This schoolyard moment reminded me that being adopted was like having a dirty secret. I thought if people knew they would think my 'real' parents had not wanted me. I feared I would be seen as less lovable than those children who were wanted. Adoption made me stand out from my peers. Something else I did not want.

When I was older I realised most people in Redland Bay would have known of my adoption, since word travels fast in a small community. My adoptive parents gave me the names of two other adoptees in an effort to comfort me.

The 1940s and 1950s was an era when adoption was seen as a 'closed' or 'secret' system and I believe that the secrecy broadcast a message of shame. Even today I recall particular anecdotes that underscored it.

Three adoptees of a similar age, including myself, attended Redland Bay Primary School for eight years but none of us ever mentioned adoption.

My adoptive family and I spent Christmas Eve and other family occasions with my parents' friends, Lena and Ray. Their adopted son, Tom, was a year younger than I and we were both mute on the subject of our adoption. We were loyal to our adoptive parents and socialised to observe the silence.

It would not be until 1994 that Tom and I had our first conversation about adoption, after my adoptive father's funeral. Tom, who was forty-five years old at the time, had recently been reunited with his birth family.

It wasn't until 2007 that my adoptive brother, Ian, and I discussed adoption for the very first time. He was fifty-seven years old. It was a brief dialogue encouraged by my name change.

Since adoption was never included in my adopted family discussions, an awkward silence on that subject fell between Ian and me. He confessed recently that this was difficult for him and that he also believed I was punished more often than he was. I was happy he eventually spoke to me of his feelings.

In the 1970s I began to discuss adoption more frequently, but my first comments were tentative because many people did not understand. I felt the guilt and did not want to appear ungrateful.

On the surface I was happy and in control, but no one knew about my inner, adoption directed life.

On one occasion, when I tried to express my feelings, I was asked, "Haven't you got over that yet?" triggering even more guilt.

I was influenced by the peer pressure of my non-adoptee peers. Society's subtle and pervasive messages were always secrecy and shame.

I remember that around this time and long before I found my birth family I frequently and subtly examined random hands and feet. I stared discreetly at passengers on buses and trams as a way of searching for my biological relatives. I have two bent fingers and two bent toes so I imagined if I found someone with that peculiarity, it was possible we were related. I sought ways like these to circumvent the negativity that bombarded me and to find connections to the people around me.

Most feedback an adoptee receives from their peers is negative. My non–adopted peers have bandied messages such as:

"I was always scared I was adopted because I didn't look like anyone in my family."

"I ran away because I thought I was adopted."

"I thought I was adopted because I was always in trouble."

"I was always scared I was adopted, because my interests differed from everyone else's."

"When I felt unfairly treated in my family, I'd scream: 'I'm adopted, aren't I?'"

Comments like these continued to shame and undermine a reluctant adoptee like me.

It was around this time in the 70s when Marie, a friend and adoptee, related a frightening experience from her childhood when some of the older pupils taunted her at school. They said her adoptive parents were going to send her back to where she had come from when she arrived home from school. I could imagine Marie's stress as she headed home that day.

Like Marie, I have two sets of parents and suffered the same confusion and division that many adoptees do. I seemed compelled to choose one parent as good and the other as bad. Then I would change my mind. My more constant decision was that my adoptive parents were good and my birth parents were bad. Researchers call the phenomenon 'splitting'. Despite this, I still have a repressed loyalty to my birth parents. This is obvious when someone criticises them.

Although researchers suggest adoptees may often see their adoptive mothers as bad, I have always seen my adoptive mother as good. I believe the adoptive mother is often seen as bad because she takes all the flak from the 'acting out' adoptee. She is at the forefront of mothering and perhaps the prime disciplinarian.

John and I started dating in 1967 and his parents learnt I was an adoptee from their next-door neighbour around that time. His neighbour was a long term resident of the Redlands and an acquaintance of my adoptive parents.

When John asked my adoptive father for my hand in marriage at the end of 1968, they had a private conversation. My father, without consulting me, revealed to John that I was an adoptee. John and I had already discussed it, so he was not surprised by the disclosure.

While I have always appreciated my father's honesty, I would have preferred to make the decision on sharing this information myself.

In the 1950s, I read a story published in *The Sunday Mail* relating the account of a wealthy family threatening to disown and disinherit their son and grandson if he married his girlfriend, an adoptee. Ultimately, the young man defied his family and married the girl he loved.

This story spoke to me at the time of the often unrealised disadvantages of life as an adoptee and the confusing issues of privacy and secrecy.

During childhood and after my adoption was revealed, I felt plagued by a lack of privacy. My adoptive father revealed a neighbour called out to him, not long after I had started school, "Have you told Jean she's adopted yet?"

I think my parents were rushed into revealing my adoption because they were worried someone else would do it for them; and being rushed to reveal one's adopted status, or having it done for me, has remained a sensitive issue.

Carolann, at nineteen years in 1967.
Photographer: the Redlands Times.

Carolann nursing her adoptive brother, Ian, in 1951.
Photographer: Bobby Gordon.

Carolann in 1952. Photographer: Bobby Gordon.

Carolann (right) with her adoptive cousin, Pam, in 1964.
Automatic Photo Booth.

Edna (Carolann's birth mother) aged nineteen in 1936
with her half-brother.

Cyril (Carolann's birth father) on the right in the 1940s.

This image of Carolann was on the front page of the Courier-Mail in 1965. Location is opposite the art college in the Botanical Gardens, George Street, Brisbane. The Courier-Mail Photographer.

12

Letters, Photos, Parcels and Endings

Though no one can go back and make a brand new start,
anyone can start from now and make a brand new ending.
– Wolfgang Riebe

1982

A letter arrived from Edna dated 6th April. I was puzzled by her familiar handwriting until I realised it was similar to mine.

> Dear Jean,
>
> Sorry it has taken so long to send your photos back. I have been searching for my snaps and at last I have found them. Could you please send them back next week as I am going away for a month next Monday.
>
> Edna

A wad of folded tissue was nestled inside the envelope. I unfolded it and extracted a miniscule portrait of a man whom I assumed was my birth father, Winston Carl Tevis. I examined his features closely. His forehead was high, his face long and lean and his brown hair was cut short and brushed back from his face. He was smiling but I could not see his eyes as he had squinted into the light. After I had examined the photo vigilantly, I determined he bore no likeness to me.

I pored over a photo of a middle-aged woman with an oval face and even features. Her figure was pleasantly rounded and she wore a smart blue dress with a red necklace. Her short brown hair was attractively styled and her face wore subtle make up. She held the hand of a tiny blond boy: Edna with her grandson, Alex.

The third photo was of a slim woman in her twenties. Her hair was thick, dark and wavy and she wore a waisted floral dress. She had her hands clasped together and smiled demurely for the photographer. I experienced a moment of intense sadness when I noticed a strong resemblance to myself.

Edna had requested her photos be sent back immediately. In 1982 photocopiers were non-existent in our district and a negative made from the image would have taken weeks. I photographed each image because a bad copy was better than nothing.

In an effort to choose openness over secrecy, I visited my adoptive mother and shared Edna's photos. She did not comment although I could see she regarded the images with interest.

The next day I posted Edna's photos back to her and the same day received a parcel containing the photos I had sent to Edna. I was delighted she had kept the duplicate. Of course she could have ripped it up.

When my phone rang, on Monday, I was pleasantly surprised to hear Edna's voice. It was the first time she had initiated contact. "I've rung to tell you not to phone me tomorrow because I won't be here for the Easter holidays," she said.

"OK," I said. "Did you get your photos back?"

"Yes, thanks. Did you get yours?"

"Yes, I did. Thanks. Well, have a good holiday and I'll phone you in a month."

The call ended swiftly when Edna's taxi arrived to take her shopping.

My family and I would move into our new home during the Easter holidays, so weeks earlier, I began the tedious chore of packing up our belongings. The month passed quickly with the move and on our appointed Tuesday, I phoned Edna.

"Hello," Edna answered curtly.

"Hello. It's Jean here."

"I'm not interested, thank you," said Edna tersely, and she clunked the receiver down.

I listened to the buzz of the dial tone. Puzzled I replaced the receiver. Edna's brusqueness shocked me. I did not know what was wrong, but I was extremely vulnerable and easily hurt.

During that day I rehashed the incident many times. Did Edna mean she was not interested in me? Did she wish to end our relationship? Shame flooded through me and my face flushed. Perhaps her brusque manner indicated someone was with her so she could not talk and if that were the case I understood. Nevertheless she could have used a softer approach.

The muscles in my stomach clenched and nausea clawed at me as the usual adoption issues of loss, abandonment and rejection placed a dark shadow in my heart. Later that day I was afraid to phone Edna in case I learnt the worst.

I persuaded myself nothing was worth the pain of more rejection. Edna had refused to meet me and denied me permission to meet my birth brother. Our relationship was nothing more than a series of phone conversations. She would no doubt be happier if I faded out of her life. My feelings were a mixture of irritation, anger and hurt. I decided I could no longer pursue such a one-sided relationship.

A few days later I contacted Edna and told her. I was unable to express my anger and disappointment and I did not give a reason for ending our relationship nor did she ask or argue.

Relief flooded through me after my phone call to Edna. At least I would not be rejected again. The next day I put it all behind me and went on with my life.

The sense of empowerment didn't last, however, when weeks later I grew doubtful of the success of my decision. Could I shut Edna out of my life forever?

13

The Farm

Life's problems wouldn't be called "hurdles"
If there weren't a way to get over them.
– Wolfgang Riebe

1982

After my family and I moved house over the Easter break, our busy farm life commenced. We employed a contractor to dredge a dam, drill a bore and install an irrigation system.

One Saturday my parents-in-law arrived to help us plant half an acre of ginger in our lower paddock.

Earlier in the year John had ploughed the upper slopes and planted 1800 banana suckers. The fruit would be dispatched weekly to markets in Brisbane and Sydney, and generate remuneration for our mortgage.

John continued to teach agricultural science at Cleveland High School, while I was fully employed as mother, housewife and farm hand. I organised our lives so we could devote all weekend to the farm. Our children built a tree house in the cool shade of the massive sixty year-old avocado tree in our back yard.

From our house we looked down on to a field that was now filled with rows of succulent ginger. Bordering the lower rim of the field were paperbark trees and ferns that prospered along the sides a gully. A creek ran through the lowest point and fed the dam.

The builders had bulldozed a site for our house, but, as yet, not a blade of grass grew. In the rainy season the red earth turned into a sticky quagmire that we had to traverse to reach the carport.

John solved the problem by laying down timber pallets like stepping-stones.

Our carport was on a higher level than the house and eventually steps were built to access it, but in the early days it was too was dirt. We bought our milk from a local source, in six litre buckets. One rainy day, whilst carrying the milk bucket, John slipped down the bank and the bucket burst open and splashed everyone. Something we laughed about for some time.

The banana plantation dominated our outlook on three sides so we were soon disgruntled with the claustrophobic setting and chopped out a large number of trees to create space for a lawn and garden beds.

On weekends we de–suckered banana trees [removed the new but unwanted plants from around the main tree] and bagged the bunches to protect them from pests. Every few weeks John slashed the grass between the rows.

In our spare time we continued to tile the floors in the family areas of the house. A small shed was built around the irrigation pumps, fortunately just large enough to use as a temporary packing area.

On weekends I drove the tractor while John chopped off the banana bunches. He heaved each bunch onto his shoulders then dumped it on the carryall. Once we were back in the shed the bananas were placed onto the floor. They were de-handed with a sharp knife, dunked in cold water to seal the sap and then placed on absorbent matting to dry. The following day we graded the hands into medium, large and extra large as we packed them for transport to the Rocklea and Sydney markets.

In September we planned a seventh birthday party for Lachlan. On the afternoon of the party we set up a large table under the paperbark trees near the dam. The geese grazed nearby while Rusty, our dog, slept under the table and my adoptive mother joined us for the happy afternoon.

Chris, aged ten, attached our trailer to the tractor and he and his friend, Angus, took the party guests for a joyride. Angus's large black dog and Rusty rode with them. Sadly the party would be the last family occasion with my mother present.

Our repertoire of crops expanded from bananas to include taro, turmeric, ginger and lemon grass. John grew one crop of zucchini, but they grew so fast it was impossible to keep up with harvesting.

In 1987, John and I planned a rose garden. We planted five hundred shrubs in long stemmed hybrid T varieties, suitable for cut flowers. We would sell the blooms at local outlets such as service stations.

A reliable young man named Sean was employed to harvest our lucrative taro crop that averaged approximately one tonne each week.

Taro is a root crop, a bit similar to potatoes, and was dug using a potato digger attached to the tractor. The taros were then collected in large bins and carted on the carryall to the shed. The next step was to tip the taros into a metal tray and rake them into a circulating steel tunnel, while water blasted away the dirt. Then they were placed on large tables to dry. The last step was to divest the taros of many small roots, using a very sharp knife before packing. A local carrying service then transported the crop to the Sydney markets.

The rose garden proved prolific and everyone in the family was involved at some time and Chris, Lachlan and Andrew earned some pocket money.

For the local market we arranged a dozen roses in a bunch interspersed with sprays of green filler [foliage], encased them in a cellophane sleeve and tied them with ribbon. We delivered them to service stations where the staff sold them on commission.

Despite the good business, the rose garden was also heavy maintenance. New blooms were cut daily and refrigerated. Blown blooms were de-headed weekly and the grassy passages between the garden beds slashed regularly. Other chores we carried out were: mulching, weeding, spraying and fertilising.

In August, each of the 500 rose shrubs was pruned back to one-third its original size.

Every now and again as we settled into our new life as a family on the farm, I thought of Edna who had been back in my life for such a short time. I had not heard from her nor made contact myself. My mind, on occasion, also strayed to my birth brother and birth father.

On the farm at Redland Bay. From left: Lachlan, Andrew, John and Chris with the bunch of bananas that won first prize in the Cleveland Show. Photographer: C. Dowding.

14

Holiday

Time goes by so fast; people go in and out of your life.
You must never miss the opportunity to tell these
people how much they mean to you.
– Wolfgang Riebe

1982

In December, John was granted one month long service-leave so we planned a trip to Sydney and Canberra. Chris and Lachlan had achieved excellent results from their respective classes so we took them out of school a week early while Andrew, now three, would stay with my adoptive parents.

Lately my mother was looking tired and I was worried about her. She complained of an odd sensation in her throat although her visit to the doctor had revealed nothing. I was dubious about leaving Andrew with her, but she protested, saying, "I would've left you with my mother, if I'd had the chance."

My adoptive grandmother had died in 1948 and my mother missed having her in her life, especially when Ian and I were children. My grandmother had stayed with us when I was a baby but died from a heart attack soon after her visit.

I came up with an idea that would suit everyone, at least so I'd hoped and told her, "OK, Mum. I'll leave Andy with you on one condition. He stays half the time with John's mother."

My mother agreed so I made arrangements with my mother-in-law. She too wanted her grandchildren to stay with her and would be happy to collect Andrew from my mother's house.

We departed Redland Bay a few days later. Our first camp was at Clarkes Beach Caravan Park, Byron Bay. In the afternoon we explored the flawless beach. Next, we moved on to Port Macquarie where the seagulls fascinated Lachlan and he fed them scraps in front of our tent. One afternoon we stopped at Wauchope, and visited Timber Town Historical Village, where we explored the old buildings and steam trains.

In Sydney we stayed at Silvan Village, Potts Point. We ventured into the city to see the Harbour Bridge, Taronga Park Zoo, Centre Point Tower, The Rocks and the Opera House.

During our stay John and I had to navigate our way through the crowded streets of Kings Cross to the train station. As country dwellers we were wary of the crowds of people in outlandish dress. We held tight to Chris and Lachlan's hands fearful they might be separated from us.

We remained in Sydney for four days and on the fifth prepared for our journey to Canberra where John's sister, Carol, lived with her husband, Colin, and daughter, Becky. We arrived at their home mid-afternoon. That night, during dinner, Carol left the room to answer the phone and returned a few minutes later with a dazed expression, saying, "Ian's on the phone. He said your [adoptive] mother's had a heart attack and been admitted to the Princess Alexandra Hospital, but her condition is satisfactory."

Oh, my poor mother! I said a silent prayer for her as I rushed to the phone and heaved a sigh of relief when I calculated Andrew would have been staying with my parents-in-law when the catastrophe took place.

John and I spent a restless night and in the morning we decided to begin our journey home.

We arrived in Dubbo at nightfall and booked into a motel. We were all tired and slept heavily. At dawn I received more bad news. My mother had suffered a severe stroke during the night. It was decided I should fly home, while John and the boys completed the journey by car.

John dropped me at Dubbo Airport where I boarded a plane to Sydney then another to Brisbane. I caught a taxi to the Princess Alexandra Hospital where I spent the remainder of the day.

I was shaken to see my adoptive mother so ill. A nurse told me the stroke had caused complete paralysis on her right side.

My mother's eyes were squeezed shut, and her skin looked clammy and deathly pale. I stood near her bed and watched her take ragged breaths through a condensation spotted oxygen mask. Another nurse informed me they had had to remove her false teeth for safety reasons. I hated seeing her in such an undignified situation.

During the next weeks I visited my mother as often as I could. On one occasion I found her with her eyes were open, the oxygen mask removed and her teeth replaced. She looked more like her old self, but she could not speak.

A few visits later a nurse provided a pencil and pad and encouraged my mother to write messages. Over the coming weeks she would attempt the almost impossible task of writing with her left hand.

One day she pointed to the pad and pencil so I passed them over. She held the pencil in a shaky hand and wrote slowly and awkwardly. When she had finished she handed me the result. "I need you," and "I thought I was at home" was scrawled on the notepad. Sadness tightened my throat as tears ran down my cheeks.

15

Passed

Join me in the pure atmosphere of gratitude for life.
– Hafiz

1983

My adoptive mother spent the next six months in a rehabilitation ward at the Princess Alexandra Hospital and participated in physiotherapy. My family looked forward to the time she would walk again and we were overjoyed when she could speak.

The hospital organised a craft group for long-term patients and during a visit, I was shown into the craft room. I spotted my mother sitting in her wheelchair concentrating on a piece of embroidery and watched her efforts for a few moments. When she saw me, she showed me the tatty material.

"Isn't this futile?" she said.

I did not answer as I did not wish to discourage her, but I understood what she meant. Before her illness she had been a skilled dressmaker. Among her achievements were gorgeous clothes and beautiful embroidery. But this – her current work – looked like a child's attempt.

Some months later, when she could stand and take a few steps and her speech had improved, my mother's doctor gave her permission to spend weekends at home. It was then that we saw how her quick wit and repartee had disappeared.

At that time, my mother's older sister, Jean, moved in with my adoptive father and brother to help.

One Sunday in May, John and I harvested bananas in a torrential downpour. I drove the tractor through the dripping banana plantation with knee-high Wellington boots filled to the tops with water. Hours later, wet, bedraggled and tired, we returned to the house for sustenance and showers.

My adoptive mother was at home that weekend and I intended to visit her late in the afternoon and bath her but my aunt phoned to explain that my mother had a cold that was worsening and had called an ambulance to transport her back to the hospital. I was disappointed but decided to visit her in Brisbane the next day.

The phone shrilled at 3.00am I stumbled to answer it in the pitch dark. I feared bad news and it was. My father told me the hospital staff had advised us to come quickly if we wanted to see my mother alive. Adrenalin seared my body. I rushed around the house, thinking of nothing else except getting to my mother's side. Outside, the rain still bucketed down.

I arranged to meet at my father's house and travel in his car with the rest of the family. I threw on clothes, ran to the carport, reversed down the short gravel driveway and swung out onto our dirt track. I accelerated to begin the uphill climb but the wheels skidded. I stepped on the accelerator, the engine roared, the wheels churned then my car veered to one side and stopped dead. I panicked, threw myself out of the driver's door, and scuttled back to the house.

A quick phone call and our plans changed.

I grabbed raincoats and umbrellas while John retrieved the tractor from the shed. It was the only way out. In the dark on that dismal morning we chugged slowly up the hill. I clung to the tractor seat with one hand, an umbrella in the other, as the machine yawed from side to side in the syrupy mud. Thankfully we reached the main road safely where my father's car was already waiting.

We sped along the forty kilometre highway to Brisbane. No one spoke.

When we arrived at the hospital, we rushed to my mother's room. My eyes flew to her bed but it was shrouded in drapes. The matron greeted us with a baleful expression and I could feel myself blanch as I listened to the sorrowing news. My mother had passed away.

The matron handed over my mother's wedding ring that had been cut in half to remove it. It was all we would take with us. We turned and stumbled out of the hospital, a broken wedding ring clutched in my father's hand.

My mother had died without our support. I was despondent. If only I had made it to her side when she needed me.

My father drove slowly home, no need to hurry now. The world felt bleak and empty.

Mary (Carolann's adoptive mother).
Photographer: C. Dowding

16

A Different Dimension

*Life is a flux, a movement. Every moment it is life changing
and becoming new. If you miss a moment you have missed.*
– Osho

1984

On the 28th April, my adoptive brother, Ian, was to marry his
fiancée, Judith, in Auckland. My adoptive father and Aunt
Jean would be attending and I was also keen to attend. After
lengthy discussions John and I decided we could afford a
holiday in New Zealand and Chris, Lachlan and Andrew
would accompany us. As an adoptee I was always sensitive,
even obsessed, about being left out of [adoptive] family events
so attending the wedding was very important and I was
determined to attend.

In the week prior to the wedding, John, Chris and Lachlan
were on school holidays. We flew to Christchurch, on the South
Island, hired a motor home, and toured for eight days.

When our holiday drew to a close, we boarded a huge
car ferry in Picton bound for Wellington on the North Island,
disembarked and travelled to Auckland.

Judith collected us and took us home to meet her family.
After a delicious dinner John and Andrew left for the airport
while Chris, Lachlan and I would remain in New Zealand to
attend the wedding.

John and Andrew returned to Australia because the
Education Department had refused John leave of one day.

Chris, Lachlan and I stayed in a beach house at
Whangaparaoa, forty kilometres north of Auckland. Judith
drove us up the coast and helped us settle in. She and her

family had very generously supplied us with groceries.

That night Lachlan became ill and vomited all night collapsing on the toilet floor after each bout. We did not have a phone or car so I was frantic.

Chris was a wonderful support and at dawn I left him in charge while I went in search of the phone box Judith had pointed out when we arrived the previous evening.

I soon found the phone box and Judith came to my rescue. Judith and her mother arrived at the beach house and we made a quick trip to the local doctor who prescribed antibiotics for a nasty ear infection.

Whangaparaoa had an interesting beach so Chris, Lachlan and I visited whenever the weather permitted. One day we caught a bus to Auckland to a museum.

When Ian and Judith's wedding day dawned, Chris, Lachlan and I travelled with friends of Judith's family. The ceremony was touching and we enjoyed ourselves at the reception. We were particularly impressed with the scrumptious wedding breakfast that included plates heaped with New Zealand oysters.

In 1985, Andrew commenced school at Redland Bay Primary School. Lachlan moved up to Grade Five and Chris enrolled at Cleveland High School for Year Eight. Chris and John would be at the same school.

I had suffered from restlessness since my adoptive mother's death. Thirty-five was a vulnerable age to lose a parent, or so I had been told. Not that any age is a good age.

At the time I had no compulsion to seek out Edna. It was never an option to replace my adoptive mother with my birth mother. They were totally different individuals and my feelings for each were diverse.

I decided I needed to do something just for me so I applied to the Brisbane College of Advanced Education to begin an Associate Diploma in Child Care. Each of my children had attended pre-school and my positive observations had swayed me to early childhood education. I had volunteered at my children's pre-school and loved the experience so I wished to replicate those times. The theory of growth and development interested me and I had enjoyed teaching Lachlan to read before he started pre-school.

I did not have a tertiary entrance score, as I had left high school after sub senior or Grade Eleven, nevertheless I could apply as a mature age student. I was required to attend an interview and take a test. I was accepted and completed the first year successfully.

John took a month long service leave and constructed a small room on the back of the house to serve as a study where I could work.

From left: Chris, Carolann, Lachlan, Ian (adoptive brother), Judith, Jean (adoptive aunt) and Jack (adoptive father) in New Zealand in 1984.
Photographer: Colin Salt.

17
Mother and Child Reunion

Well I'm forty now Mum
Long time no see…
To have actually known you should be enough
But what I really miss is the twinkle of a smile
In your eyes
And the awesome agony of a tear coursing down your
Cheek.
– Shelton Lea, *'Poem from an Adoptee'* from The Love Poems

1987

I was now thirty-nine years old. Five years had passed since my last contact with Edna.

One morning John and I took a leisurely drive and ended up near Loganlea so we decided to do a drive-by of Edna's house.

John drove up her street, turned the car around and parked on the opposite side. I looked back at her house and glimpsed a woman in the window pulling the curtains closed.

"I think I saw Edna."

"Go in and see her," said John.

I delayed for a few seconds then made a snap decision.

"OK. I will."

"I'll stay here," said John.

I checked my makeup and raked my fingers through my dark curls. As I crossed the street I smoothed down the full skirt of my mauve and white sundress and thanked my lucky stars I had worn something decent.

I moved swiftly to keep up my momentum and when I reached Edna's steps I took a deep breath and climbed. I arrived at the top step too quickly and my heart began to beat faster. I hesitated and then knocked firmly. A few moments later I heard a scuffle inside then the click of a lock and the door began to open slowly.

A woman in her early seventies stood there. Her short wavy hair was almost white and combed back from her forehead in an attractive wave. She was my height with a rounded figure and wore a cotton shift in a tiny flowered print. If the woman was Edna she did not recognise me. She smiled and her hazel eyes lit up.

"Yes?" she said.

"Hello. I'm Jean," I answered.

The woman looked stunned and hesitated for a moment. "Oh! You'd better come in then."

I then knew the woman was Edna. We looked into each other's eyes and smiled. Her eyes 'mirrored' mine exactly and when she smiled the resemblance was incredible. The irises of our identical hazel eyes were edged with the same bluish grey line. Just like Lachlan's eyes too.

Edna reached out and hugged me and I hugged her back. I could hardly believe it. I had not expected physical affection. She seemed a different person to the one I had spoken to five years ago and I assumed she must have had a change of heart.

Edna held me away from her and looked at me closely. "Oh," she said, "You've got such beautiful skin."

"Thank you."

"I love you," she said, surprising me.

"I love you too," I mumbled.

"I'm just in an old house dress," she said. "I'll just go and change into something better."

"It doesn't matter," I said, although she went anyway.

My eyes scanned the room. Everything was neat and clean. A television set, placed across the far corner, was switched on with the sound muted, and the inexpensive furniture was arranged in comfortable seating. I noticed a pair of gardening shoes near the back door and realised our feet must be similar as they were worn in similar places.

Edna smiled as she walked back into the room in a different outfit.

"My husband's waiting for me in the car," I said.

"Tell him to come in."

"Are you sure?"

"Yes."

I skipped down the steps and invited John to join us. I introduced him to Edna and she offered us morning tea. I helped her prepare it and noticed her super tidy pantry. I had inherited the neatness gene.

John, Edna and I sat at her dining table and persevered with conversation. It was complicated. We had no background information to help our discussion and certain subjects were taboo such as my birth, birth father, adoption or adoptive parents.

My birth brother, Bill, his wife, Marnie, and their son, Alex, were some of the topics Edna introduced. We described our farm. An hour or so later I kissed Edna goodbye and promised to call again.

I smiled all the way home. I think I was happy.

Edna's behaviour was a complete contrast to five years earlier, but I did not question her because I did not wish to upset things.

I wondered if Edna regretted her initial negativity towards me. To see me, for the first time since I was one month old, would have been confronting for her. She was given a second chance to welcome me and she had done it superbly.

During this time, I completed my Associate Diploma in Childcare and was relieved and proud when I received my certificate in the mail.

In November, we held an eighth birthday party for Andrew. He chose a small group of special friends and we had a pleasant afternoon.

In 1988, Lachlan transferred to Grade Eight at Cleveland High School. Now Lachlan, Chris and John would be together.

Early in the year, a colleague from the Brisbane College of Advanced Education opened a childcare centre only twenty minutes from my home and offered me a job as the group leader in the pre-school room. The hours were marvellous so I accepted.

I met my friend Marie at the childcare centre. We had common interests because she was also a group leader and an adoptee. Our conversations regarding adoption led me to thoughts of Edna, and I had a strong compulsion to visit her again.

At the end of my first year I decided childcare was not for me although I had enjoyed teaching pre-schoolers. The childcare centre closed in mid-December for the Christmas holidays, and I handed in my resignation on the last workday.

18

First Visit

In every trial let understanding fight for you.
– Buddha

1989

John, Lachlan and I arrived at Edna's house. Lachlan was thirteen and he and Edna were total strangers. Being introverted they found it difficult to bridge the age and stranger barrier.

Edna offered us morning tea and we accepted. I suggested she might like to visit our home someday and she seemed pleased. She and I parted on good terms.

On the home front, I enrolled in portraiture classes to extend my folio as I intended to apply to Griffith University to study fine art. I had acquired a tertiary entrance score from my studies at the Brisbane College of Advanced Education.

Chris graduated from Cleveland High School and began a Civil Engineering degree at the Queensland University of Technology.

John took two months long service leave to extend the tiny sleep out at the back of the house for Chris. John and I designed a long desk that would stretch the width of the room. Chris sold potted native plants and bunches of roses and saved up to buy a second hand Toyota Corolla panel van. The vehicle needed a new engine so he and John carried out the mechanical transformation themselves.

Lachlan received awards for academic excellence in Grade Nine. Previously he had been chosen as vice-captain in Grade Seven at Redland Bay Primary. When he graduated from Cleveland High School, Lachlan undertook a Bachelor of Engineering Aerospace and Avionics.

Andrew, who had been vice-captain at Redland Bay Primary School, graduated and enrolled at Cleveland High School.

During 1992 I assembled my art folio and resumed my application to Griffith University. I was then requested to attend an interview and take a drawing test. The day of the interview I was shown into a studio with nine other applicants. I noticed a large shrouded object in the centre of the room. I chose an easel quickly and set out my equipment just minutes before a lecturer swept into the room and unveiled the mystery object.

Everyone gasped at the strange assemblage we were expected to draw. It was an assortment of junk topped off with an overturned plastic chair, a potted umbrella tree and a roll of scrunched up carpet. I and the other applicants were seriously challenged to make this into a beautiful drawing. Adrenalin flowed and I drew intensely. When time was up and we handed over our signed drawings, I thought of Edna and how I had inherited my drawing ability from her and the German artist back in the family tree.

And I had done it. I had passed the drawing test.

It was a matter of weeks before I would be informed that I was accepted into the Griffith University art program.

Edna (Carolann's birth mother) on the right with friends in the 1960s. Photographer: family member.

Carolann in 1992 picking roses on the farm at Redland Bay.
Photographer: Judith Gordon.

John on the farm at Redland Bay in 1992.
Photographer: Judith Gordon.

19

A Reunion, Lie and Revelation

As long as the ignorance of the self lasts
so long will there be misery.
– The Tripura Rahasya

1992

I knocked on Edna's door. She was her usual hospitable self and asked us in. John and I sat on the couch, while Edna took a single chair and we chatted for a few minutes before I spied a large pair of gym shoes pushed under one of the chairs. I was intrigued. Did Edna have someone living with her? During our conversation my eyes constantly flicked to the mysterious shoes. I said, "I'd love to know more about my biological family."

"Oh you don't need to know all that," said Edna. "Relations mean nothing. I never see any of mine these days."

As usual Edna dominated any discussion linked to adoption and birth relatives. I am sure she had good reasons, but she had a habit of totally disregarding my questions.

"I'd like to know more about my medical history too." I persisted. "Doctors always ask."

My lack of medical information niggled at me. Although I knew a little of my maternal medical history, I knew nothing of my paternal and I was sick of explaining this to doctors. Studies show that adoptees worry about unknown conditions they might pass on to their children and I was no exception.

I observed Edna and noticed she seemed perturbed as she sat and stared into space.

"Tevy's [Edna's son, Bill] left his wife," she blurted out. "He's living here now so you can't stay long, he might come back any minute."

"He's not at work today?"

"No. He's on holidays."

I glanced at the doorway half scared half hopeful of my birth brother's imminent arrival.

"Those shoes must be his?"

"Yes. He might come back any minute so you'll have to go," stressed Edna.

"Couldn't I meet him? I mean if his marriage has already broken up?"

"No. I couldn't tell him now. He's too upset," said Edna.

I had played the game Edna's way for ten years by then, and quite out of the blue, she moved the goal posts. Back in 1982 she said Bill's marriage might break up if he found out about me. Now it had and it had nothing to do with me. Besides, during such a stressful time for Bill, discovering he had a sister might have been a good diversion from his marital problems.

Still, I saw that Edna's fear was palpable. I was frustrated and annoyed but empathised with her dilemma. I indicated we should leave and we stood and said goodbye.

On the journey home my face flushed and my chest tightened. Edna had virtually tossed us out of the house.

When we arrived home I was disturbed.

"Do I have the right to meet my birth brother?"

"I don't know, but I don't think Edna's being fair," said John.

"Why should Edna's wishes outweigh mine? We should be equal."

I made lunch for us and while we ate my thoughts raced. Then suddenly I made a decision. "I've made up my mind. I'm going to phone Bill."

"Good. I think you have the right."

But I had a problem. Bill lived with Edna.

"Imagine if I phoned Edna and asked to speak to Bill?"

"It's not worth considering," laughed John.

A few days later, I nervously dialled Bill's workplace.

"Stegbar," answered a male voice.

"Hello. I'd like to speak to Bill McBroom, please."

"Sorry. He's on holidays."

I thanked the man, hung up, and absorbed my disappointment. I had no idea when Bill's holidays would end.

Another week passed before I considered contacting Stegbar again.

In the meantime, John offered to drop in to Stegbar, as he would be in Brisbane for a school sports event.

Later that day I waited on tenterhooks. Finally I heard John's car rumble up the driveway and I rushed out to meet him. He shook his head as he walked towards me.

"No luck. I went to Stegbar but he's still on holidays."

I decided to try Bill again on Monday.

Monday morning I called Stegbar and a man picked up after a couple of rings.

"Hello, I'd like to speak to Bill McBroom, please."

"He's down in the work room, but hang on and I'll go and get him," said a friendly male voice.

I thanked the man and began a nerve-racked couple of minutes. Finally I heard the rustle of paper before someone picked up the receiver.

"Hello, Bill McBroom speaking," said a genial male voice.

"Hello, Bill, my name's Jean Dowding. You won't know me, but I've something to tell you which might be a bit of a shock."

Silence.

"I was adopted in 1948 and the documents show Edna Doris McBroom is my birth mother. I have my original certificate I can show you."

Silence prevailed then at last, Bill spoke. "This isn't a total surprise, you know. I've always suspected something like this because my grandmother told me I had a little sister but she'd had to go away."

"Why did she tell you that?"

"I'd often ask why I couldn't have a brother or sister. Mum always said she couldn't have any more children. Anyway she would never discuss the past, but one day when Mum was out, Grandma told me."

"I contacted Edna ten years ago but she said I mustn't tell you."

"Oh you should have told me sooner. Secrecy is ridiculous in this day and age. Nobody cares about things like that anymore. Anyway I'm pleased to have a sister. What about your birth father? Did Mum say anything about him?"

"Apparently you and I have the same birth father."

Bill's acceptance was encouraging. Friendly and communicative, he put me at ease. I couldn't help but recall the contrast of my first difficult phone conversation with Edna.

"We'll have to meet soon," suggested Bill.

"Yes, for sure. Would you like to come to my house?"

"I've always loved the railway house at Ormiston," said Bill. "I was happy there and over the years I've returned several times to check it out. We're both connected to it so it'd make sense to meet there. I'll come to your place afterwards."

"OK. I'll bring my adoption documents. Later, you can meet my family. Would you like to stay for dinner?"

"Yes, thanks."

I asked about what to serve because Bill might have been a vegetarian for all I knew. I suggested lasagne.

"I can't eat raw tomatoes, but cooked are fine," he added. "How about we meet next Sunday?"

I agreed we would meet at the Railway cottage at 2.00p.m.

During the week I felt the usual butterflies but I knew meeting Bill was something I had to do on my own. What would he think when he saw me?

As Sunday drew closer I explained my plans to my children. They were intrigued by the thought of meeting their [birth] uncle.

Sunday dawned a fine autumn day. The cloudless sky was phthalo blue and sunlight sparkled on the sea. Our rondeletia shrub had recently burst into flower and its perfume permeated every corner of the garden. I felt light hearted and exhilarated because I had stepped out from under Edna's control.

I baked lasagne and prepared a salad. After lunch I dressed carefully in dark violet slacks and a long sleeved white blouse with large coloured glass buttons. I applied makeup and tidied my short wavy hair.

John hugged me and wished me well before I drove off in our Holden Kingswood, my adoption documents lying on the passenger seat.

The drive took twenty minutes and I slowed down as I approached my destination. I spied a shiny maroon vehicle parked on the verge, pulled in behind it and climbed out of my car. At the same time a man emerged from the other car and walked towards me holding a bunch of flowers. It was a heart stopping moment as he smiled and handed me the flowers.

Bill was tall and dressed in casual clothes. He had wide shoulders and an athletic build. I imagined he played sport or had in the past. His wavy brown hair was sprinkled with grey, his forehead high, and his cheekbones wide. He had grey eyes and when he smiled he exuded a pleasant demeanour. I noticed Bill resembled Edna in one way as he had the same distinctive gap between his two upper front teeth.

Bill was forty-seven years old and I was forty-four and according to the natural order of things, we should know each other but instead, we were complete strangers. We hugged quickly and pecked each other on the cheek awkwardly. He suggested we sit in his car so I grabbed my folder eager to begin our conversation.

Bill turned and looked at my face.

"I see a strong resemblance between you and my mother," said Bill.

His words put a warm glow into my heart, instilling a sense of belonging. And I was intrigued. Edna had said I did not resemble anyone.

Bill spoke of my birth cousins and my likeness to some of them. I handed him my adoption documents and watched as he perused them silently, thoughts of imposters creeping, unwelcome, into my mind.

Bill pointed to my birth date.

"We couldn't possibly have the same father," he said.

"Couldn't we? Why is that?"

"Well, you were born early in 1948 but my father returned to America in 1944. All the Americans had gone by the end of 1945."

"Are you sure?"

"Yes, quite sure."

I was shaken and wondered what on earth was going on. Another so called truth was violated. My heart pounded and a swishing sound pulsated in my ears. Had I believed a monster lie for ten years?

"Edna said we had the same father, an American, named Winston Carl Tevis," I said. "She even sent me a photo of him."

I shuffled through my papers and pulled out the blurry copy of my birth father's photo and handed it over.

Bill studied it carefully.

"I don't know if that's my birth father or not," he explained. "It seems to be a different photo to the one I've seen. By the way, his name is Carl Winston Tevis, not Winston Carl. My second name is Carl."

"I don't understand. Why would Edna lie? Why swap the names around?"

I related Edna's account of the death of my birth father from a cerebral haemorrhage, while he was working on the railway lines. I told him about the nasty letter from the parents, blaming her for his death. I had assumed my birth father died in America but now everything had changed. My insecurity escalated.

"I don't know that story," said Bill. "My birth father worked as a mechanical engineer for the air force. I'm sure he never worked on the railway lines. The only part of your story that corresponds is that my father died."

"I'm so confused," I moaned.

"Mum and I hid from someone once. I think it was something to do with grandparents who she thought were going to take me away. Of course I was very young so I may have got it wrong."

Bill explained that Edna's older brother, Alfred, had been a friend of his birth father's during the war. It was he who told Bill his father's identity.

"I wonder who my birth father is," I said.

"I don't know, but I'll get in touch with Uncle Alf. He's been a father figure for me all my life. He might know something."

"Oh thanks. I wouldn't be game to confront Edna and accuse her of lying, Bill."

"From now on you'll have to call me what everyone in the family does," said Bill.

"What's that?"

"Tev. Everyone calls me Tev."

I returned to my car and led the way back to Redland Bay. Tev met my family. We had afternoon tea and then strolled around our farm. Tev and I posed for photos. The family dinner was a success and he promised to see us again soon.

In the days following, my heart was filled with happiness, but my joy did not last long when I recalled Edna's lies and the fact she had duped me for ten years. Anger surfaced and I burnt with a strong desire to find out the truth.

During the next weeks I thought deeply about my next move. Because my adoption certificate was already in my hands, I had never bothered to apply to Family Services for my original birth certificate, or the identifying and non-identifying information.

I knew the laws had changed and adoptees were now entitled to more information. I was curious to know what Family Services would come up with so I sent in my application.

A few weeks later Tev arrived on a Saturday afternoon with a bundle of photo albums. We pored over them for hours as he acquainted me with my maternal birth family.

My maternal grandmother, Martha Siemsen, was born in Brisbane of German immigrants. They moved to Pittsworth then took up farmland nearby at Stoneleigh.

My maternal grandfather, Friedrick Fechner, was also born in Brisbane of German immigrants. His family also took up farmland at Stoneleigh.

Martha and Friedrick, my maternal grandparents, met and their marriage took place in the Pittsworth Methodist church on 8th February 1912.

I had never been to Pittsworth so I looked forward to a future visit to see the town and locate my ancestor's graves. Our close friends, DiAnne and Bob, had lived in Pittsworth for five years, but at that time I had no idea my ancestors were part of its history.

Tev explained he planned to visit Uncle Alf in Moura during the Easter holidays and we were optimistic he would have information about my birthfather. Tev assured me he would phone as soon as he arrived home.

Weeks passed but Tev did not phone. John and I were surprised because he had seemed so enthusiastic. Was something wrong? I was reminded of the frustrating time in 1982 when I waited for Edna's phone call. I wondered if he had found out something that had turned him against me. I was immensely relieved when he called and arranged a visit.

As it turned out, Uncle Alf knew nothing about my birth as Edna had successfully kept it a secret from her siblings.

Uncle Alf had since contacted his brothers and sisters and between them they had come up with a list of four putative, or possible, birth fathers: (1) Pat Murphy (2) Cyril Carlyle (3) Dan Jefferies (4) Arthur Pooley.

Tev also had a surprising story to tell me. Edna resigned from Queensland Railways on 12th July 1952. I would have been four and a half years old and living at Redland Bay with my adoptive parents. Tev would have been seven and a pupil at Ormiston Primary School.

After her resignation Edna and Tev moved to Ipswich to live with a man named Pat Murphy. He was a widower who worked as a stonemason and had a son, Gary, a few years older than Tev.

Before Edna and Pat cohabitated, his wife had committed suicide, but it was hushed up. Was Edna 'friendly' with Pat before his wife's suicide? I had no idea, but apparently Edna and Pat had been acquainted for years. Before they moved to Ipswich Tev remembered Pat visiting them at Ormiston.

Edna and Pat's relationship deteriorated during the next few years. He was a heavy drinker and became abusive. When she had put up with enough abuse, she applied for police protection to leave the relationship. She was pregnant and procured an abortion.

Then on 1st November 1954 Edna rejoined Queensland Railways based at Thorneside in the Redlands district.

Tev and I returned to our conversation about putative birth fathers.

"I can't believe Pat Murphy's your father because you're nothing like him either in looks or personality," said Tev.

Apparently Pat's hair was red to sandy and his skin freckled. Neither had Tev noticed a resemblance to him in my three children. Tev classed Pat as a truly horrible man.

"At least by being adopted you were spared association with him," he added. He told me that Pat Murphy had died in 1991 and in his opinion, it was good riddance.

Later in the week John and I looked up Murphy in the phone book and found Gary in Ipswich. He was possibly, but not very likely, my birth brother. I was happy my birth occurred early in 1948 because it did not seem the right time line.

Edna never revealed anything about her live-in relationship with Pat Murphy. Did she think I would judge her? She gave me the impression she had cohabitated with only two men, her husband, Edwin McBroom, and Tev's father, Carl Winston Tevis.

One day not long after Tev's visit I had an unexpected phone call.

"Hello, is that Jean?"

"Yes."

"It's Uncle Alf, Edna's brother, speaking. I'd like to welcome you to the family."

I thanked my uncle and then he asked me to send a photo of myself as he might see a likeness that would help him identify my birth father.

Uncle Alf and his wife, Anne, had nine children. He kindly offered to send me some old photos of Edna and some of his immediate family.

"Now I have to help you find your birth father," said Uncle George. "I've talked to my brothers and sisters, and we've come up with four possibilities. The first is Pat Murphy. Edna lived with him in 1952."

"Yes, Tev told me. He doesn't think he's my birth father as we're totally different in looks and personality."

"The second is Edna's friend Dan Jefferies. They met when she was stationed at Calvert around 1955 to 1956. Jefferies was a married man who lived in Calvert during the week and returned home to Ipswich on the weekends."

"I would have been seven years old then," I said.

"No, it's doubtful he's your birth father," agreed Uncle George.

Edna's association with these men surprised me. She always portrayed the image of a woman who had led a chaste life. In her youth she was extremely attractive, so I had been told. As a single mother she would have been particularly vulnerable as a young, unattached female and a drawcard for men.

"The third possibility is Cyril Carlyle. Edna's half-brother, Ben, worked with him at Queensland Railways in Ipswich in the 1940s. Cyril was a porter on the Ipswich-Boonah line. Ben remembers Cyril and Edna going to the theatre together."

"Cyril sounds like a possibility. Where did Edna live when Cyril worked with Ben? Where would they have met?"

"I'm not sure but Ben said he'd be happy to talk to you. I'll give you Ben's and my brother-in-law, Kev's, phone numbers. Kev was a train driver on the Ipswich-Boonah line so he might remember Cyril."

"The fourth possibility was a man named Arthur Pooley. He was a friend of Tev's father and visited Edna after the war."

I took notes as we talked. Uncle Alf imparted a feeling of security and I was very grateful for his input.

"My daughter Rosemary lives in Rosewood and I've asked her to give you a call sometime," said Uncle Alf.

According to Tev, Uncle Alf, hated secrets and lies.

A few weeks later I received a letter and photos, including some of Edna.

Dear Jean, John and family,

I am sending some photos; hope they will be some value to you. I have more old snaps to look at and may find some more.

The roses are nice, and also yourself. It was a good snap of John about to punish the digging folk. You and John have three good-looking sons.

When you write back let me know what name you were before marriage.

Cheers for now and I hope everything will turn out for the best.

Love from,

Uncle Alf & Aunt Anne

So! I had four putative birth fathers. John and I looked up the phone directory for the surnames Jefferies, Carlyle, Murphy and Pooley.

Cyril Carlyle was not listed in the Brisbane phone book so we examined electoral rolls for all states. No luck. John listed phone numbers for the other Carlyle residents in Brisbane, 'Carlyle' being a relatively uncommon name.

One day John and I drove to Ipswich to view houses owned by anyone named D. Jefferies. It did us no good. Progress would not be possible without more information.

In the following week I received my non-identifying and identifying information from Family Services. I was now the proud owner of my original birth certificate but right in the centre was a notice stamped in red: Not To Be Used For Official Purposes.

Birth Certificate [excerpt]

Name: Carol Ann

Birth Date: 18th January 1948

Birthplace: Queen Street, Cleveland

Mother: Edna Doris McBroom, formerly Fechner, age 30 years

Father:

My birth father's information was nil, but I noted a paragraph in my non-identifying information that alluded to his occupation.

Family Services had supplied a list of thirty-five possible occupations recorded under the following heading: General Category - Labourers and Related Workers. What pitiful information and certainly a deterrent for a curious adoptee, but possibly a useful tool for cross-referencing. Six of the thirty-five listed occupations were: Railway Labourers, Ushers and Door attendants, Luggage Porters, Storemen, Freight and Furniture Handlers, Guards and Security Officers.

Included in my information was the following statement from Family Services:

We can only release information on the birth parent that signed your adoption papers.

That parent was Edna.

Edna's occupation was listed under the heading: Managers and Administrators. At the time of my birth, Edna was a station mistress, who was thirty years old, married, of Protestant religion, and located in the outer city area. Details such as eye colour, hair colour, height, weight and complexion, birth father, or anything else of interest were non-existent.

I noticed a statement under the following heading: General Comments.

I gasped when I read: 'Your mother had a son in 1945, whom it appears, remained in her care. He was not a child of her marriage. You and your brother do not appear to have the same birth father. There is no record of any special interests or hereditary traits.'

At last I had written proof Edna had lied about my birth father being the same person as Tev's birth father. Family Services knew we were illegitimate. I assumed they must have our fathers' names recorded.

I was desperate to speak to someone so I dialled the Adoption Hotline. A female officer answered and I hastily gave my name and adoption number, ACR 6315, because adoptees have a number just like a prisoner. I conversed for a few minutes then applied a bit of pressure.

"Family Services are aware my birth brother and I have different birth fathers so you must have the names of our fathers recorded," I said. "I shouldn't be denied the name of my birth father. It's not fair Family Services know my personal information."

"I'm so sorry, Jean, but we can't release that information as your birth father didn't sign the adoption papers," explained the officer. "I know you are hurting. There are many people out there just like you and we have the greatest sympathy for you."

Frustration! Employees of a government department are permitted to know personal information that I am denied. And they have the right to withhold it. Family Services should be obligated to release birth parents' names. How nonsensical to keep records if they are never used!

My conversation with the Family Services officer continued.

"My birth brother's father is Carl Winston Tevis, isn't he?" I said.

"Something like that," said the officer. "We have more information on one of the men than the other."

"Why would that be?"

"I don't know. Maybe your birth mother liked one of the men more than the other."

I was stunned. I hung up and sat for a long time staring into space. My heart thumped and my body shook. How would I overcome this hurdle?

It was clear adoptees were treated as second-class citizens. They were refused rights that non-adoptees take for granted. I noted the way society set up certain boundaries and if the adoptee tries to step outside those boundaries, restraints came into play very quickly.

A few days later I phoned Ben, Edna's younger half-brother, and asked him about Cyril Carlyle. Ben was a gem. His personality was helpful, communicative and friendly and he sincerely empathised with my predicament.

"I knew Cyril really well," said Ben. "He and I worked together as lad porters for years. He was a hard worker and nice to talk to."

"What did he look like?"

"He was tall with dark curly hair and nicely dressed," explained Ben. "A funny thing though, he had a gap between his two upper front teeth, just like Edna. He wore his hair in a different way, for those days, as it always seemed to hang down across one side of his forehead. I lost touch with him when I changed jobs, but I definitely remember Cyril and Edna going to the theatre together."

I thanked Ben for his help and he invited John and I to visit him and his wife Sylvia, on his acreage at West Ipswich.

John phoned Kev, Uncle Alf's brother-in-law, the retired train driver, but he did not remember Cyril Carlyle so I knew the next step was confront Edna.

I dialled her number.

"Hello."

"Hello, Edna, I need to talk to you about something important. A few weeks ago I applied to Family Services for my adoption information. I'd like to read a paragraph to you."

"Yes, OK," Edna said quietly.

I read from the material: "Your mother had a son in 1945, whom it appears remained in her care. He was not a child of her marriage. You and your brother do not appear to have the same birth father."

I waited for Edna to speak, but dead silence wafted down the line. I waited a few more moments and then I queried her. "Well, is it true? Do Tev and I have different fathers?"

"Yes," whispered Edna.

"Who was my birth father?"

Edna did not answer. The moments of silence multiplied and the tension was thick.

"I was raped," she whispered in a husky voice.

I quaked at Edna's revelation. I was stunned, shocked and horrified. An image of a dirty rough escaped prisoner pierced my reality. I imagined him holding her at knifepoint as he forced himself on her. Eventually I managed to speak. "Oh that's terrible," I muttered. "Did you report it?"

"No. You wouldn't bother back then," said Edna.

"Where did it happen?"

"In the cottage at Ormiston."

"How?"

"I'd seen him on the platform a few times. One night he knocked on the door and asked to use the phone. I let him in, then, you know, it happened. Tev was a little boy asleep in the next room so I didn't want to make a fuss and wake him so I just let it happen."

"What did he look like?" I asked.

"He was tall, nice looking with dark curly hair and well dressed."

"Was he Australian?"

"Yes."

"Did you know his name?"

"No," said Edna. "I'd only seen him on the platform a few times."

I did not know what to believe. Was Edna telling the truth? "But you must have known his name because Family Services know his occupation," I argued.

"Oh I just ticked anything," replied Edna.

Edna and I ended the phone call on uneasy footing. During the day I reviewed her story again and again. My stomach cramped and I felt shaky. Could I believe her? She had concocted a fantastic yarn in the past.

As the day wore on I felt very alone. I had no one with whom I could discuss this. I looked forward to when John would arrive home from work to be with me. What had been a glorious sunny day now seemed gloomy.

How would I cope with Edna's astounding revelation? Should I even believe her? I had opened Pandora's Box and did not like what I had found.

If for some obscure reason, Edna were reticent to divulge my birth father's name, rape solved that problem. One can always say she did not know a rapist. If the story was true, why had she not told me ten years earlier when I first inquired? Why all the subterfuge about an American birth father? Nothing made sense.

I wondered if my birth father – the tall, well dressed, nice looking Australian with dark curly hair – caught the train regularly in Ormiston. It was a tiny community in the 1940s so everyone who lived there would have been acquainted.

I spent the next few weeks in a fit of depression. Whether Edna's story was the truth or a lie I could not find peace. Would I be able to continue my search for my paternal birth family? If she was to be believed, I had reached the end.

20

Out

Wisdom consists in speaking and acting the truth.
– Herakleitos

1993

The story of Edna's rape often played on my mind and I approached the mystery of my birth father in an analytical manner. What did I know about him? I kept repeating the details Edna relayed to me: a tall, well-dressed, nice-looking Australian with dark curly hair.

Family Services declared my birth father's job was within the category of Labourers and Related Workers, including Railway Labourers, Ushers and Door Attendants, Storemen, Luggage Porters, Freight and Furniture handlers, Guards and Security Officers; but Edna said she had just ticked a box.

I reviewed my notes from my conversations with Edna's brothers, Uncle Alf and Ben. Did Edna's description fit their description? Yes, Ben's description of Cyril Carlyle was a match.

I needed to unearth Edna and Cyril's whereabouts for April 1947 when I was conceived.

What if Edna was already pregnant when she arrived in Ormiston and had lied about the location of the alleged rape? I would need the exact date Edna took up her position as the station mistress at Ormiston in 1947.

John and I often discussed the challenge of unearthing Edna's movements but I realised that if I could view Edna's railway employment records, I could find the answer.

The Railway Historical Centre was located in Ipswich.

I phoned and asked about viewing Edna's records. They informed me I had permission if the employee had resigned twenty years earlier. Edna had retired only fourteen years ago, but it was still possible to view her records if I had Edna's permission to do so. Drat! She would never consent to that. I despaired.

What was I to do? My brain worked overtime for days. Gradually through the brain fog a plan evolved. I'd give it a try anyway.

I typed a letter to the Railway Historical Centre and requested copies of Edna's employment records for family history purposes. I requested to receive the information at my address. It worked.

For an extra fee the Railway Historical Centre would do searches and personal questions. I applied for the start and finish dates of Edna's transfers throughout the thirty-one years of her employment. I also asked for information about Edna's parents, Martha and Fred Fechner. Then I waited.

One weekend, John and I visited the Railway Historical Centre where we accessed Cyril Carlyle, my putative birth father, and Edna's brother Ben Lovell's records.

Cyril John Carlyle was born on 5th December 1927, revealing a ten-year age gap between them. In 1947, Cyril was only nineteen years and Edna twenty-nine.

Cyril was employed as a porter on the Ipswich-Boonah line from 1944 to 1948. On 12th December 1948, he was promoted from a porter to a shunter. He resigned from Queensland Railways on 18th June 1949.

Edna's records arrived from the Railway Historical Centre and I examined the contents meticulously.

On Edna's record card was the following statement: 'Deserted by American Husband, one son born in 1945.'

Edna's first job with Queensland Railways was at Munbilla. She started work as the station mistress on 23rd January 1947 and lived in the railway cottage nearby.

Six months later, on 26th July 1947, Edna was transferred to Ormiston. Wow! My suspicions were correct. I was conceived in April, so when she moved to Ormiston she would have been three months pregnant.

I had proof Edna had lied again. I was not conceived in the railway cottage at Ormiston because Edna was not there. The alleged rape must have occurred at Munbilla. When she saw my birth father on a railway platform it must have been at Munbilla not Ormiston.

Edna did not own a car and had never learnt to drive so it was unlikely she would have been in the Ormiston railway cottage at night in the month of April. Anyway another railway employee resided there at that time. Her tale was full of lies!

Where in the world was Munbilla? I asked John. Bingo! Munbilla was half way between Ipswich and Boonah on the rail line Cyril Carlyle traversed every day. What a coincidence!

Cyril and Edna had been work colleagues. He as the porter would have disembarked and she, as the station mistress, would have interacted with him.

Edna must have had her reasons to hide the identity of my birth father. Could she have been embarrassed by the ten-year age gap? Whatever the reason, to ensure the cover-up, she had deceived me again.

At this point, I was convinced Cyril Carlyle was my birth father. All the facts pointed that way.

I phoned Tev and told him about Edna's alleged rape and the information I had received from Family Services.

"When I asked Edna my birth father's name she said she couldn't tell me because she'd been raped."

"My mother was never raped," scoffed Tev.

"You don't think?"

"Mum would never let a man push her around. She's always been as strong as an ox physically and mentally. I remember a tale, and it's legendary. She punched a man in the face at a dance when he made an unwanted pass at her. There's no way she was raped," laughed Tev. "I've heard of women crying rape if they wish to hide something."

I explained the alleged rape must have occurred at Munbilla not Ormiston, according to my research, which caught Edna in another lie.

I needed the truth and was resolute I would find Cyril and ask him.

During our recent visit to the Railway Historical Centre, John and I found historical data relating to the closure of the Fassifern Valley, Ipswich-Boonah railway line.

An image of the last goods train, steam engine C 17 No. 253, leaving Munbilla on 27th June 1964, the eve of the line's closure, accompanied the article.

In the photo we noticed the tiny Munbilla Station and on the opposite side of the line was a small cottage. It was most probably the cottage in which Edna had lived in 1947.

Back on the home front I put my family research aside and concentrated on my university studies. Everyone in my family was busy in 1993. Chris, Lachlan, and I were full time at university and Andrew was in his first year at high school.

Sean, our permanent labourer, had resigned so we employed casual labour on the farm. John continued to teach full time and work hard on the farm. Our mortgage was paid off and he hoped to resign soon and become a full time farmer. The banana plantation was demolished and in its place, we grew ginger, taro, yams, cassava and roses.

I kept my acquaintance with Tev from Edna. When time permitted I did more research on Cyril Carlyle and applied to the Registrar General's Department for two birth certificates. They offered the following information:

Birth Certificate [excerpt]

Name: Cyril John Carlyle:

Birth Date: 5th December 1927

Birthplace: Lady Bowen Hospital, Brisbane

Father: John Carlyle, aged 24

Mother: Ethel Mary Carlyle [nee Allardice] aged 20

Birth Certificate [excerpt]

Name: Edna Doris Fechner:

Birth Date: 7th December 1917

Birthplace: Ellenborough Street, Ipswich

Father: Johann Freidrich Fechner

Mother: Martha Henrietta Minnie Fechner [nee Siemsen]

It was now clear Cyril had resigned from Queensland Railways in 1949 and vanished. Was he dead? John researched cemeteries in Queensland while I applied to the Registrar General's Department for notification of Cyril's death in ten-yearly sequences. I was informed that he had not died in Queensland.

John phoned a Carlyle from our 'to do' list. He spoke to a woman who said Cyril might have been someone in her husband's family a long time ago. She suggested we phone again to speak to her husband. We did not make that call, though years later, it was clear that we should have.

Carolann's artwork, 'The First Biological Relatives She Met Were Her Own Children', portrays the obsessive need of many adoptees to connect to their genetic relatives. Photographer: C. Dowding.

Carolann (left) and her adoptive cousin,
Donny, at Redland Bay in 1950.
Photographer: Bobby Gordon.

Carolann Carlyle Dowding

Carolann's artwork 'D.N.A.' stresses the importance of
this modern scientific phenomenon.

Carolann (alias Jean Gordon) with the Redland Bay Juniors in 1952. Carolann, in the second row, fourth from the left and her adoptive cousin, Donny, front row, in the centre. Redland Bay State School Photographer.

Carolann's artwork, 'Loss', relates to issues of loss and isolation that are often experienced by adoptees. Photographer: C. Dowding.

From left: Carolann holding one of Biddy's puppies, Lyndal a school friend,
Ian (adoptive brother) and Pam (adoptive cousin) at Redland Bay in 1955.
Photographer: Bobby Gordon.

Carolann's artwork,'Identity', makes a statement about the many
identity issues that affect adoptees. Photographer: C. Dowding.

From left: Donny, Leon and Pam (Carolann's adoptive cousins), Carolann and Ian (adoptive brother) at Redland Bay in 1959. Photographer: Bobby Gordon.

Looking towards Stradbroke Island from Redland Bay. Photographer: Lesley Bullen.

Carolann (alias Jean Gordon) and her adoptive brother, Ian, at Redland Bay Primary in 1960. Redland Bay State School Photographer.

Carolann's artwork, 'Jigsaw Sky', comments on the information adoptees must piece together to find their genealogical background. Photographer: C. Dowding.

21

Another Passing

Even death is not to be feared by one who has lived wisely.
– Buddha

1994

It was a big event when Chris, a Civil Engineering graduate with honours, secured a job with engineers Leddy, Sergiacomi and Associates in Hervey Bay. John and I accompanied him to Hervey Bay to find a place and eventually rented an old holiday cottage at Point Vernon with a million dollar view. A week later we travelled back to Hervey Bay with a trailer and two cars loaded with his things and stayed ten days to help Chris settle in.

Halfway through the year Lachlan decided to change his university course to Information Technology and took six months to work on the farm.

I attended university part time. In the second semester I dropped a subject to give me more free time.

At this time, my adoptive father was diagnosed with terminal prostate and bone cancer. His doctor explained the medical implications at a family conference where we learned he had only a few months to live.

My father was a hardy soul and pottered around his farm most days. He had lost a lot of weight and his back ached during the winter months. He asked me to sew him a woolly wrap with ties that would secure it firmly around his torso. I did and he was very grateful and wore it under his clothes every day.

Sadly my adoptive father passed away on 6th September, Ian's birthday, at eighty-two after a short bout with pneumonia.

He died in his own home with his family at his bedside.

A few days before the funeral we attended a private open casket session. I took the opportunity to have a little joke and tucked a packet of his favourite cigarettes and a box of matches into his coat pocket. He always enjoyed a good laugh and would have appreciated the gesture.

During the following months, John and I missed my father. We expected him to turn up at any moment for one of his unannounced visits when he would sit in a comfy chair on our verandah, drink a cup of tea and have a good chat. Inevitably he would smoke one of his Craven A cork-tipped cigarettes.

John told me a story. "One day when I was sick in bed and everyone was out, Jack drove up, walked onto the verandah and knocked on the front door. I didn't answer as I was too sick and I hoped he'd go away.

"Jack sat for ages in his usual chair on the verandah and lit a few smokes. Eventually I decided I'd better drag myself out of bed and go and speak to him. When I appeared on the verandah, out of the blue, he got an awful fright."

My father's will was read and Ian and I inherited our father's land and money. Ian and Judith inherited the main farms and the old family home. I inherited my father's two-bedroom cottage and a five-acre block of land.

I decided to sell the cottage to Ian and Judith because my father had asked me to give them first option if I sold. It was a practical solution as the cottage adjoined their land.

When the sale was finalised, I purchased a building block, with a view across Moreton Bay, in the Orchard Beach estate at Redland Bay. John and I planned to build a new home in a few years.

One day, Tev brought his son Alex to meet us. Chris, Lachlan, Andrew and Alex were first cousins but complete strangers. Under normal circumstances cousin relationships begin in childhood and the bonds are strengthened at recurrent family gatherings, but this gathering was a first for all of them.

Alex was a cheerful and communicative young man who had enjoyed a close relationship with his grandmother, Edna.

He commented on my likeness to her. "Your mannerisms remind me so much of Grandma. Wouldn't it be great if we could all have Christmas together someday?"

I thought Alex's suggestion was wonderful but deep down, however, I did not hold much hope.

Not long after Tev's visit, Uncle Alf's daughter, Rosemary, contacted me on a Sunday afternoon. She was the first birth cousin I had spoken to and we chatted compatibly for some time.

Months later I had the opportunity to meet Rosemary when John and I travelled near Rosewood. I called her on my mobile and she told us she was available and happy to have us visit. We had fun sharing family likenesses that included dark hair and high cheekbones and a similar body build, although I was taller. I met Rosemary's youngest child, a dear little boy, whose birthday was the same date as mine.

In 1995, Chris moved from Hervey Bay to Bundaberg to work in the firm's main office. Lachlan began his degree in Information Technology and sailed through his studies. John applied to the Education Department for extended leave without pay, and began his journey toward becoming a full-time farmer. I still faced the mystery of my missing birth father, one of my priorities in the New Year.

22

Still Searching

We can live without religion and meditation,
but we cannot survive without human affection.
– Dalai Lama

1996

Chris moved back to Brisbane to start a new job with engineers John Wilson and Partners and we were thrilled to have him closer to home.

Edna still remained unaware of my acquaintance with Tev. I was wary of her reaction if and when she found out. Obviously guilt, anger, fear and secrecy were unfortunate side effects of adoption, and we were each affected in our own way.

John and I visited Edna in the New Year. At the end of our visit, as I kissed her goodbye, I asked her a question that was often on my mind.

"Can you tell me my birth father's name?"

"I can't tell you or it might all start up again," Edna said clearly.

I was astonished. Edna had finally admitted there was a reason she refused to divulge my birth father's name. It was something I had always suspected. Of course I was fairly certain who he was, but I wanted to hear it from her lips because Edna was the only person who knew the truth of my birth father's identity.

"Oh, I've ruined everyone's life," moaned Edna.

I was intrigued. Edna had not mentioned rape this time around; it was a totally different scenario. I interpreted her words as meaning: 'I know your birth father's name, but I'm too scared to tell you because something might start up again'. I had no idea what that something might be.

As a result of my reticence, nothing more was said about the past and Edna and I bade each other goodbye.

Edna proclaimed she had ruined everyone's life. In what ways I could not imagine but I assumed that because of my relinquishment, I was one of those people.

I contemplated Edna's confession and it led me to believe that deep down she carried a great deal of guilt and I was jolted out of my previously held assumptions of her character. Researchers often write of the crippling guilt birth mothers experience after relinquishment. I realised she had not escaped unscathed and my feelings towards her softened.

During the next few weeks I applied for four certificates from the Register General's Department. They contained the following information:

Birth Certificate [excerpt]

Name: William Carl McBroom

Birth Date: 22nd May 1945

Birthplace: Brisbane Women's Hospital

Mother: Edna Doris McBroom (nee Fechner), aged 28

Father: Not Recorded

Tev's birth certificate was similar to mine because his father was not recorded. Tev's father had returned to America eight months before he was born.

Marriage Certificate [excerpt]

Names: Edna Doris Fechner, aged 24 years to Edwin McBroom, aged 28 years

Date of Marriage: 5th December 1942

Place of Marriage: West End

Usual Residence of Bride: Walloon

Usual Residence of Groom: Amberley

Birthplace of Bride: Ipswich, Queensland

Birthplace of Groom: Urania, Louisiana, United States of America

Birth Certificate [excerpt]

Name: Ethel Mary Allardice [Cyril Carlyle's mother]

Birth Date: 5th April 1907

Birthplace: Queen Street, Jubilee Estate, Enoggera

Father: Thomas Wingate Allardice, aged 22 years

Mother: Lily Allardice, nee McDonnell, aged 21 years

Death Certificate [excerpt]

Name: Ethel Mary Carlyle (nee Allardice) [Cyril Carlyle's mother]

Age at Death: 26 years

Date of Death: 20th October 1933

Cause of Death: 1. Burns to arms and legs 2. Bronchi Pneumonia 3. Heart Failure

Issue: Cyril John, 6years Alma Ethel, 4years

Married for 7 years to John Carlyle

Sadly my putative paternal grandmother, Ethel Carlyle, was only twenty-six years old at the time of her death. What sort of an accident could have caused such a tragedy?

I noted Ethel was born under the astrological sign of Aries, with her moon in the sign of Capricorn. Coincidentally I was born under the sign of Capricorn with my moon in the sign of Aries. We had the same astrological signs only in reverse.

I have been told that astrologers believe biologically related individuals often have the sun, moon or rising sign [ascendant] in the same astrological signs although not necessarily in the same order. My putative grandmother's astrological signs, repeated in my horoscope, created greater hope that the Carlyle's were truly my birth relatives.

So the search for my birth father continued.

The Salvation Army ran a free investigative service and their philosophy was to bring families together. The only fees they requested were expenses from the Registrar General's Department and other sundries. I applied, but a gracious woman regretted they could not help me because Cyril's name was not on my birth certificate. Ethel Carlyle's death certificate revealed that her son, Cyril, had a younger sister named Alma Ethel. I decided to search for her. As she was not listed in the phone directory I assumed she was married. I applied for Alma's marriage certificate for a ten-year period including the ages of nineteen and twenty-nine. A few weeks later I received a disappointing result: Alma Ethel Carlyle had not married during that time.

That year, December brought many changes. Lachlan received his Bachelor of Information Technology in Computing Science with Distinction. Andrew graduated from Cleveland High School and applied to study Information Technology at Queensland University of Technology. I passed my art subjects and John enjoyed a more relaxed lifestyle as a full time farmer. John and I also hitched our caravan to the old Land Rover and travelled to the Sunshine Coast for ten days. Lachlan and Andrew stayed home.

The oceanfront at Mooloolaba was a welcome change of scenery and the roar of the surf lulled us day and night. On most early mornings, I searched for seashells and found numerous kauris in mint condition, an astonishing occurrence on such a busy beach.

One Saturday afternoon Chris arrived at our caravan and introduced us to his girlfriend Kerryn, a cheerful, articulate and intelligent young woman. We dined in the caravan on home cooked fish and chips and enjoyed an amicable night.

The year was over and I did not know where the search for my paternal birth family would lead me, but I intended to persevere in the New Year.

23

A Birth Family Reunion

Our prime purpose in this life is to help others.
and if you can't help them, don't hurt them.
– Dalai Lama

1998

The New Year heralded more changes in our family. Andrew commenced his degree in Information Technology and Lachlan secured a position as a computer programmer in the Information Systems Department of Queensland Rail. His office was in the inner city so he caught the train from Cleveland, as did Andrew. Very early on Saturday 6th June the phone shrilled.

"Hello Jean, it's your [birth] cousin, Rosemary, here. My sister, Annette and I would like to invite you to a family reunion."

Rosemary explained the reunion was for my maternal ancestors, the Kruger's.

My [birth] great-great grandmother, Anna Dorothea Kowalski, married Johan Kruger in Germany in the mid-1800s. She was widowed then migrated to Australia in 1884 with a large family. Anna's daughter, Emilie, was my great grandmother. Emilie's daughter, Martha, was my grandmother.

"When's the reunion?"

"Today, in the Croquet Hall at Queens Park, Ipswich," said Rosemary. "It starts at 10.00am. A café is nearby or you can bring a picnic lunch."

"It sounds interesting. Yes, I might come."

"Annette would love to meet you and Aunty Edna's sister, Aunty Fran, and her brothers, Bob and Ben, will be there. Your [birth] cousin, Darren [Aunty Fran's son], is going too. It'd be a great chance to meet them."

"Thanks, Rosemary. I'll see you in a few hours."

I asked John if he would come and we rushed to get ready and prepare a picnic lunch.

We arrived at Queens Park just after 10.00a.m. and I noticed Rosemary, and a woman I assumed was Annette standing near the hall. John and I hurried over and Rosemary introduced us. Annette had blond hair and was shorter than Rosemary. They were both very friendly and their eyes twinkled with mischief when they suggested introducing me to my birth relatives. I deduced they were out to have a bit of fun and hot to introduce Edna's daughter to all the unsuspecting relatives. I must admit I was delighted to be part of the fun.

Annette and Rosemary whispered to me, "That's Uncle Bob [Edna's brother] over there." They ushered me forward.

"Hi, Uncle Bob," said Rosemary. "I'd like you to meet Aunty Edna's daughter."

"Hello. Pleased to meet you." I smiled and reached out to shake his hand.

Uncle Bob's eyes bulged. Then he screwed up his face and blurted, "It's Edna reincarnated."

Rosemary, Annette and I laughed.

"Here comes Aunty Fran, Edna's sister," whispered Rosemary. "Come over here and meet Aunty Edna's daughter, Aunty Fran," she called.

I smiled and said hello.

Aunty Fran's face fell and she turned pale. "I didn't know she had a daughter!"

We conversed for some time and John photographed us. In due course Aunty Fran drifted away with a worried expression on her face.

The fact that I was at the reunion soon became common knowledge and more relatives made their way towards me. Roy Jenkins, Edna's brother-in-law, introduced himself.

Ben [Edna's younger half-brother] introduced himself and his lovely wife, Sylvia. They were pleasant, friendly people just like Ben's phone manner had suggested. Ben pulled me aside to speak privately. "When I saw you today something about your looks jogged my memory. It's about Cyril Carlyle and Edna. Give me a ring next week."

"Thanks, Ben. I will." Such excitement. I hoped his information was good.

Rosemary and Annette introduced us to my birth cousin, Darren. His occupation was as an Engineering Draftsman so we explained our son Chris was a Civil/Structural Engineer. We talked companionably and exchanged phone numbers. We were all amazed when we realised John had been Darren's stepson's teacher at Cleveland High School.

John and I enjoyed the reunion immensely. We had the chance to peruse ancestors' photos and ancient wedding certificates in a relaxed environment.

Helen, a distant birth cousin, was the reunion organiser and had written a history of the Kruger family. The manual would be available in a few months at a reasonable cost. I enthusiastically added my name to the order list. Group photos of different descendants were taken and I was elated to be included.

John and I joined Annette, Rosemary and Aunty Fran for lunch at a long refectory table in the hall. We tucked into our food and chatted at the same time.

"Would you tell us who Jean's father is, Aunty Fran?" said Annette unexpectedly.

Aunty Fran flushed. "I don't know."

Everyone was silent for a few minutes.

"Edna had a terrible time, you know," stated Aunty Fran as she looked pointedly at me.

"I know she did but it's not my fault," I said.

No one argued with my statement. Nothing more was mentioned about the past and when lunch was over we dispersed.

A couple of hours later John and I thanked Rosemary and Annette for including us and said goodbye. As we turned to leave Rosemary grabbed my arm. "You are like Edna you know, but much nicer," she whispered.

Somewhat embarrassed I thanked her for the compliment.

A few weeks later I wrote to Rosemary and Annette and thanked them for inviting us to the reunion. I received warm replies from each of them.

I reminisced about the family reunion and wondered what the outcome would have been if Edna had turned up.

During the next week I phoned Ben as he had requested. He discussed the 1940s when he and Cyril Carlyle worked together for Queensland Railways in Ipswich. He also mentioned an anecdote about Edna and Cyril.

"In 1947 I was still living at home. One day, when I was in the garden, I overheard my mother make the following comment to someone in the kitchen '…it was Cyril Carlyle who got Edna pregnant'."

I gasped.

"A few days later my mother cornered me and asked if I knew Cyril Carlyle and, if I did, what I thought of him," said Ben. "She said she was interested because apparently he wanted to marry Edna."

"Wow! Thanks for that, Ben. It's proof Cyril is my birth father. Edna wouldn't tell me my birth father's name but she did describe him and it fits your description of Cyril so this makes so much sense."

I thanked Ben again and hung up the phone. I was sure he was trustworthy. He had given me his sister [Edna's younger half-sister], Gail's, phone number. One day I plucked up the courage to phone her. She sounded like a lovely person, and was happy to talk, although she knew nothing about my birth or adoption.

During the coming weeks I basked in the happy afterglow of the Kruger family reunion but also envisaged Edna's reaction to my attending the reunion. I was sure Aunty Fran would have told Edna as soon as she arrived home and shuddered to think how angry she would be. On a positive note at least my maternal birth family knew I existed.

One year would pass before I overcame my trepidation and visited Edna again.

Helen, my distant birth cousin and author of the *Kruger Family History*, contacted me. Some months earlier I had discussed family history with her over the phone and sent copies of relevant birth and death certificates.

Helen explained her plan to protect the 'oldies', meaning Edna, in the manual. Edna would be protected by listing her as the mother of two children, but Tev and I would not be mentioned by name.

I was terribly disappointed. Helen did not wish to include my name in the family history manual because the old adoption taboos were still rampant. If I had been Edna's adopted daughter, I would have been eligible for entry. As Edna's birth daughter, I was not. Tev's and my descendants would never make it into the Kruger Family History Manual.

Why was Tev excluded? He had always been in the family. Perhaps Helen had compromised. Maybe she did not wish to hurt me and thought it would be easier for me if both of our names were left out.

Regardless, it did hurt. I am included in the family history records of my adoptive family, even though my name is bracketed (adopted). It didn't make sense not to be included in the family history records of my birth family, the place where I belonged genetically.

24

Making up

Love and compassion are necessities not luxuries.
Without them humanity cannot survive.
– Dalai Lama

1999

For the first time since the Kruger family reunion, I walked up the steps on to Edna's verandah. We had not seen each other or spoken for one year. She emerged from the living room and reached out and hugged me. I hugged her back.

She said, "I was very angry with you."

"I was very angry with you too," I answered.

"I didn't want things to end up as they have between us," said Edna.

I nodded and smiled. What could I say? I did not understand my own reactions; far less someone else's.

Edna and I did not discuss the reasons for our anger, but I assumed hers had been linked to my 'outing' at the Kruger family reunion the previous year.

Edna invited John and me into her home and the three of us enjoyed a relaxed conversation. She always showed interest in our farm. I guess it was a safe topic. Our relationship was back to normal.

A few months later I learnt Edna, who was now eighty-two years old, was in the Princess Alexandra Hospital with arrested circulation in her lower leg and foot. Her doctor had mentioned possible amputation.

I walked into Edna's hospital ward, but she did not recognise me for a few seconds. Later she told me she was thinking, "Who is the beautiful lady in the red dress coming to my bedside?" I was touched by her compliment and thanked her. We had a pleasant visit.

Fortunately Edna did not have an amputation. Medication and physiotherapy relieved her circulatory problems and she was discharged after a few weeks. She was a smoker and had been told to give up or at least cut down. I believed she chose the latter option.

The downside of Edna's stay in hospital was the loss of Arlie, her adored pet dog. He disappeared one day, never to be seen again. He was a pedigree Staffordshire Bullterrier so she believed that someone stole him. Edna was heartbroken. She had treated him like a child, fed him on chicken breast and sewed him a soft padded bed. I commiserated with her on the loss of her pet.

Back at home, things were changing. Redland Bay had become a popular residential area and numerous housing estates were evolving so John and I subdivided our farm. We tussled with the local council and spent many months dealing with red tape until everything was approved.

Our son Chris designed the engineering works and we sold to a land developer. At the end of the year we engaged an architect to design a house for our block of land in the Orchard Beach Estate. We accepted a quote from a suitable builder and early in December the first clods of earth were turned over.

John was offered a position as a part time horticultural workplace trainer for Technical and Further Education. His work often took him near Loganlea and he would visit Edna occasionally. Of course he always took a packed lunch and she would make him a cup of tea. He said she seemed to enjoy the company.

In effect she was his second mother-in law. A lot of men would have cringed at the thought!

Was Edna still unaware of our relationship with Tev? During one visit, John decided to break the silence and discussed Tev as if he had always known him. Strangely Edna showed no surprise. How long had she known? I supposed the fiasco of my attending the Kruger family reunion had led her to expect the inevitable and I was grateful it was out.

John and I met Tev in 1992, and it took eight years for our relationship to come out into the open. John's initiative had solved the stalemate.

Carolann (left) aged forty in 1988. Her birth mother, Edna, aged thirty-two in 1949. Photographer: Judith Gordon.

25

Freedom of Information

We ourselves feel that what we are doing is just
a drop in the ocean. But the ocean would be less
because of that missing drop.
– Mother Teresa

2000

I attended university part time. Andrew began an innovative university program in which he worked part time for Dialogue, a designated Information Technology firm. His degree would take another year but after graduation he was guaranteed a full time job.

Our house at Orchard Beach was completed by the end of June and John, Andrew and I moved in. The view dazzled us but we found the road noisy after living on the farm.

Lachlan elected to remain at our farmhouse and pay fifty dollars a week board while we took care of power and phone bills. He lived alone for a few months then asked permission to live there with his girlfriend, Joanne. They were twenty-five years old and had dated since Grade Eleven so we were happy to acquiesce.

Over time, we discovered white ants devouring the radiata pine used for our extensions at the farmhouse. A huge nest was also found in the dividing wall between the laundry and kitchen and another in the hall. Lachlan and Joanne swore they heard the ants crunching during the night.

At the end of the year Lachlan and Joanne moved out and the demolition team moved in. John videotaped the occasion and later I walked across from the Orchard Beach estate to inspect the damage. Our house and garden was scattered across the scarred earth. The next day the mess was bulldozed into a huge heap, loaded on trucks and carted away to the rubbish tip.

We were sad. We spent eighteen years in that house and our children had grown up there. Machinery demolished it in one day.

Tev informed me Edna had fallen on her steps and was hospitalised. Consequently Social Services deemed her high house unsuitable and recommended she move into care or live with Tev. His current house was one story and would be appropriate with extensive alterations to the bathroom and toilet.

John and I visited Edna before she moved and found her unwell and distressed because her shopping was overdue. We offered to take her and help with the groceries. It was the only time we shopped together. She asked us to stay for lunch and I helped her prepare sandwiches. We worked well as a mother and daughter team.

"We would have been OK. It's just that we've lived different lives," said Edna.

I liked that statement and took note of the positive impact it had on me. To date my relationship with Edna had been awkward and unpredictable. She was right. We had lived different lives. Although my adoptive parents loved me, I also needed affirmation from Edna so any positive comments were extremely welcome. I was thrilled she thought I would have been acceptable in my biological family. I was so pleased our relationship was growing.

Edna had recovered from her fall and Tev undertook some renovations to make his home more comfortable for her.

As time passed I became aware of the right of adoptees to have more information. I was curious and applied to Freedom of Information. Six weeks later a large envelope arrived in the mail. Four documents of were of particular interest:

STATE CHILDREN DEPARTMENT: APPLICATION TO ADOPT A CHILD.

No. 18966

Adoption Order Number ACR 6315

Mary Isobel and John Ivor Gordon, residents of Redland Bay, wish to adopt the infant Carol Ann McBroom, resident at Redland Bay, the child of Edna Doris McBroom.

The infant was born on the 18th January 1948, at Brisbane Women's Hospital, and is a British subject who has never been married.

2. STATE CHILDREN DEPARTMENT:

Infant life Protection Act

HISTORY FOR INVESTIGATION: Date: 20 -1-1948 No. 18966

MOTHER: Edna Doris McBroom, a married woman, aged 30, the daughter of Martha Fechner/Bell of Walloon and Fred Fechner (deceased)

Address: Ormiston

Mother's Occupation: Station Mistress

CHILD: Carol Ann

Born: 18 - 1- 48

Where: Brisbane Women's Hospital

PUTATIVE FATHER: (Mother will not divulge)

Address:

Father's Occupation: PORTER (RAILWAY)

EVIDENCE: Is there any proof of paternity? Yes

(a). By Letters? Yes (received on 27/1/1948)

REMARKS - Nice baby - medium colouring.

3. DISTRICT REGISTRAR'S OFFICE: BRISBANE WOMEN'S HOSPITAL

Date: 20 -1-1948 No. 18966

I have this day received notice under the 17th Section of *The Infant Life Protection Act of 1905*, of the birth of an illegitimate child under the age of five years.

Birth Date: 18 -1- 1948

Birthplace: Brisbane Women's Hospital

Name of Child: Carol Ann McBroom

Name of Mother: Mrs Edna Doris McBroom

To: The Director of the State Children Department

4. WARD OF THE STATE: No. 18966 Carol Ann McBroom

A WARD OF THE STATE! I could not believe it. How could I equate the life I had led to a 'ward of the state'? Humiliation! Orphanage! Such thoughts brought me back to earth with a big bump.

Edna was probably coerced by the powers-that-be to register me as a ward of the state.

Authorities knew Edna was already the mother of one illegitimate child and in the 1940s such mothers were watched rigorously. They took a tougher stance if a woman gave birth to two or more illegitimate children. If, after intense scrutiny, the authorities disagreed with the quality of care the children received, they could remove them from their family of origin.

My thoughts returned to Document 2. My birth father's name was absent and 'Mother will not divulge', was written in the blank space.

I noticed my birth father had sent a letter to the authorities to claim paternity, received on 27th January 1948, nine days after my birth. On the tenth day Edna and I were discharged from hospital.

In Document 2, my birth father's occupation was recorded as railway porter: more proof for Cyril Carlyle, a porter.

I phoned the Freedom of Information hotline in a state of excitement and suggested they could verify my birth father's name from the letter he had written to the authorities in 1948 claiming paternity.

The officer gave me some upsetting news. The letter, along with many other documents, had been destroyed in the 1974 floods. Only information previously transferred to microfiche had survived the disaster.

I was astounded. Why on earth had they failed to transfer my birth father's name from the letter to microfiche? The letter had been in their possession since 1948. Something so vital should not have been overlooked. I had anticipated seeing proof of paternity in my birth father's handwriting and the chance to possess something personal. My mood was low after that depressing piece of news.

Eventually I brightened up and contemplated the positives. At least my birth father had cared enough to write and declare paternity. Would a rapist write to the authorities and claim paternity? Probably not.

It was December and almost Edna's birthday. I noticed she displayed a framed portrait of Tev at about eighteen months so I decided she should have one of me at a similar age. I found an attractive red frame with a tiny decorative carving on each side and posted the gift and card promptly.

A few days later the phone rang. It was Edna. She seemed quite excited and thanked me for the birthday gift. I was amazed she had phoned. It was the second time only in eighteen years.

Matha Henrietta Minnie Siemsen
(Carolann's birth maternal grandmother).

26

Family Occasions

*Truth is by nature self-evident. As soon
as you remove the cobwebs of ignorance
that surround it, it shines clear.*
– Mohandas Ghandi

2000

Edna often talked about my birth cousin, Susan, who, Edna informed me, was also adopted. Apparently she phoned Edna frequently and visited when possible. Did Susan know I existed? Surely Edna would have mentioned me. I hoped she had.

I phoned my birth cousin, Darren, and we chatted. Before we hung up I asked for Susan's phone number. If she had not heard of me I determined to put her straight. Late one morning I dialled her number.

"Hello."

"Hello, is that Susan?"

"Yes."

"You won't know me Susan. My name's Jean Dowding. I am Edna's daughter."

"What?"

"I can tell from your reaction you didn't know about me. Edna gave me up for adoption when I was two weeks old. She named me Carol Ann. You and I have a lot in common as we are from the same biological family and we're both adopted."

"I'm not adopted," said an indignant Susan.

Shock. Silence.

"Oh, I'm so sorry. Edna told me you knew."

I could not understand why Susan had denied she was an adoptee. Tev and Edna had often mentioned it.

Susan and I continued to converse and then the subject of Edna came up again.

"I look quite a lot like Edna," I said.

"I look like Edna too," said Susan.

"But I think my nose is a little different to Edna's," I added.

"Oh! When Aunty Edna was a teenager she had an awful accident. She tripped on a railway line and a splinter of wood pierced her nose."

"I heard about that. It must've been painful."

"Yes. Poor little bugger," said Susan.

"I inherited my drawing skills from Edna," I added.

"I can draw," said Susan.

"Can you?"

"Yes, I can draw a straight line," she guffawed.

Susan seemed taken aback and I assumed she was trying to save face by making a joke out of the situation. I was sure she did know about her adoption since to find out as an adult would be a terrible shock. Maybe she was in denial?

Tev mentioned that he and other family members thought Susan looked like Edna. It seemed she thought so too.

Out of the blue I had a sneaking suspicion. Perhaps she thought Edna was her birth mother. It would explain her negative reaction to my sudden appearance.

"Do you think Edna is your birth mother?"

"No. Oh I don't know," mumbled Susan.

Susan was ambivalent. I could tell she was unconvinced I was Edna's daughter.

"I was born in January 1948. When were you born?" I asked.

"July 1947," said Susan.

"You're only six months older than me so Edna couldn't possibly be your mother could she?" I said kindly.

Susan was quiet for a few moments.

"No, I suppose not."

Silence.

"Well then, who is my mother?"

Our conversation was bizarre. Should I share the information that Edna and Tev had shared with me? Should I tell Susan her birth mother's name?

"Aunty Fran is your birth mother," I answered.

"Oh!" gasped Susan, "the worst mother you could have!"

Susan's reaction to Aunty Fran was because of an incident that happened many years previously when Aunty Fran and her husband broke up and he forbade her to see her children. Consequently she was estranged from them for some time.

My conversation with Susan continued.

"You could apply for your adoption information from Family Services, you know. You're entitled to your original birth certificate. I could help you."

"Oh no, I don't think so. I'd rather not know."

Susan's outlook was valid. Some adoptees do not wish to know and it is their choice.

I mentioned the Kruger family reunion in Ipswich.

"What reunion?" Susan asked. "Why wasn't I told?"

"I don't know," I answered.

Susan and I talked about family names. I mentioned McDonald, my mother-in-law's maiden name.

"Old McDonald had a farm e-i-e-i-o," sang Susan in a silly voice, then laughed heartily.

I forced a small laugh. Our conversation was fast coming to an end. Before I hung up I gave her my phone number and suggested she stay in touch.

"Don't be a stranger, eh?" she answered.

My revelations would have been a surprise, if not a shock, so a few weeks after our initial conversation I decided to phone Susan again. A man answered the phone.

"Yeah," he answered in a gruff voice.

"Hello, could I speak to Susan please?"

"Who is this?" the man demanded.

"Jean Dowding."

The man was silent for a moment.

"Are you something to do with Edna?"

"Yes," I answered indignantly, "I'm her daughter."

"Well," sneered the man. "We don't want any of your shit here. You piss off."

I was astounded. My hand froze around the receiver. Neither of us hung up and I waited in silence with the receiver clamped to my ear.

"I'm still here," I said.

"Well, you'd better piss off then," growled the man and he slammed the phone down.

"That went well," I mumbled as I placed the receiver down. My body started to shake. I wasn't used to verbal abuse.

I decided not to contact Susan again.

Many months later I heard from Tev. Apparently my birth cousin Susan and her older brother, Trevor, thought I was an imposter. What a laugh. Why would anyone bother?

A bit later, during one of Trevor's yearly visits, Tev showed him copies of my adoption certificate and photos to prove that Edna's daughter did exist, however.

It was then that I began to understand that reunions were fraught with unknowns. I was an interloper in my birth family and could understand their reticence when someone new entered their lives and threatened the status quo. Their wariness was understandable. I was grateful most of my birth relatives were amiable and courteous and welcomed me into their world.

During this time, Andrew moved into an inner city unit with two other students, convenient to his work and university, launching John and me into the empty nest syndrome. We had a big house now, but it was too late. They had flown!

John and I visited Tev and Edna again and after afternoon tea Tev took John to see his new carpentry tools. Edna and I talked companionably for a few minutes or so.

"Come into my bedroom. I've something to show you," said Edna.

She led the way and I admired her neat, clean room and her pretty bedspread. She discussed some of her favourite possessions and then offered to lend me her used Mills and

Boon novels. I searched her room for my photo in the red frame but I was disappointed. I did not ask. I thought it better not to know.

"Look at this," said Edna.

She pushed a small cardboard box towards me, lifted the lid and removed a wad of tissue that she placed carefully on the bed. She peeled open the tiny package and disclosed a sliver of wood about two inches long, discoloured on one end with a dark substance. She picked it up gingerly and held it up to the light.

"That's the splinter that pierced my nose when I tripped on the railway line. That stain is my blood," stated Edna. "Afterwards my nose was never the same."

Edna gave me a detailed account of her accident and subsequent trip to the doctor.

"It must have been excruciating," I said.

"Yes," said Edna. "It certainly was."

I assumed Edna must have talked to my birth cousin, Susan, recently. Susan and I had discussed her accident on the railway line. Edna did not mention Susan, and I was too cowardly to bring up my phone call to her. Again, secrecy prevailed and I harboured annoyance that Edna had not told Susan of my existence.

Edna and I returned to the living room and then she suggested we sit on the front patio. I decided it was a good opportunity to ask some pertinent questions. "What was my birth father's name? I wouldn't try to trace him or anything, but I'd like to know more about my medical history."

Edna turned and glared right into my eyes. Anger oozed and her pupils turned to pinpricks. "Well, you can't anyway," she snapped.

We sat in silence for a few minutes then Edna said, "My sister never knew her father and she's OK."

I thought, but there is one big difference. Edna's sister knew who her father was! She also grew up in her biological family.

Edna's lack of understanding of an adoptee's plight was infuriating. I assumed she could not cope with any negativity because it reflected badly on her.

I decided aggression would not work so I put my arm around her shoulders and stroked her arm. I was too spineless to mention Cyril Carlyle, but maybe I could cross a few other putative birth fathers off my list.

I disregarded Edna's hostility and audaciously asked some more questions.

"Was Sam Lovell [Edna's stepfather] my birthfather?" I asked.

"No," said Edna as she shook her head. "He was a bastard, that's for sure, but he didn't do that."

"Was my birth father Patrick Murphy"? [The man had Edna lived with in Ipswich in 1952].

"Who?"

"Pat Murphy," I stated clearly.

Recognition dawned in Edna's eyes.

"No."

Just then John and Tev returned and I ceased the questions.

One fine May afternoon, Chris and Kerryn married in the Roman Catholic Church at Albany Creek. Kerryn's pretty blond hair, dark brown eyes and lovely complexion were shown off to perfection in an off the shoulder full-length dress with shoestring straps and embroidered bodice. She carried a bouquet of white tulips.

Chris looked handsome in a crisp black suit, tulip buttonhole, and white shirt that suited him. His dark hair was short and his green/grey hazel eyes sparkled with happiness.

John and I were touched to witness the marriage of our first-born child. The reception started later on the terrace at the Clear Mountain Resort where nature provided a colourful sunset.

In six months Chris and Kerryn planned to go overseas to Ireland where they intended to work for a year. Chris later wrote an account of their adventures in his book, *A Few Drops Short of a Pint*, and published with Interactive Publications.

In June, John and I toured Thailand with our friends, Joy and Jack. The tour was organised as an exotic gardens tour for nursery owners, John and I being the exceptions. We explored many superb gardens in north and south of the country. In Bangkok we trawled the Chattachuck markets where we inhaled numerous smells, some good and some bad. I was sad when I saw squirrels for sale, their legs, tied to the counters with string.

Our Thai tour guide escorted us to restaurants where the food was delicious. We also toured temples, ancient buildings and the war cemetery.

The highlight was a trip on antediluvian train. It travelled the line built by prisoners of war in World War Two. We poked our heads out the open windows of the timber carriage and felt the warm air on our faces. I glimpsed the famous River Kwai flowing through a steep ravine and later our group visited Kanchanaburi and walked across the bridge over the River Kwai.

Edna was interested in our trip to Thailand. She and her friend, Bert, had holidayed in Singapore a few years before. During the war Bert had been a prisoner in Changhi Jail.

Back on the home front, Chris and Kerryn departed for Ireland. John and I were sad to see them go but excited to read the emails that arrived regularly. In December, Andrew travelled to Ireland and spent Christmas with Chris and Kerryn and then toured the countryside including Northern Ireland and Belfast.

John and I spent Christmas in Adelaide after towing our caravan from Queensland. The spectacular Great Ocean Road was a highlight of our journey.

Carolann and John at the bridge over the River Kwai in Kanchanaburi
Thailand in 2001. Photographer: J. Drane.

27

Keep Trying

Never give up, for that is just the
place and time the tide will turn.
– Harriet Beecher Stowe

2000

Along this journey, 'Keep Trying' became my motto.

I had dabbled in astrology since the late 1970s and longed to have an accurate horoscope configured, but I needed my exact birth time, and as an adoptee that is not so easy.

In 1980, I heard that the local medical centre, Redlands Clinic, stored the records from the now defunct Cleveland Hospital so I inquired about viewing my birth records. No luck. The receptionist explained records, more than ten years old, were destroyed the previous year.

In 1982, when I first contacted Edna, I asked about my birth time. Around 2.00a.m. she said.

In 1992, Tev said he was born at 2.00am. I thought it extremely unlikely we had the same birth time and doubted the accuracy of Edna's recall. Nevertheless I had my birth chart professionally configured although I was never convinced of its accuracy.

During a difficult childbirth Edna was transferred from Cleveland to the Royal Women's Hospital in Brisbane in 1948. Perhaps my birth records were at the Royal Women's.

I phoned the hospital.

"There is no way you, or anyone for that matter, would have access to birth records," said the receptionist.

Ten years later, in an optimistic mood, I phoned the Royal

Women's again. A polite receptionist transferred me to the 'new' Customer Service Department where another staff member assured me I could receive photocopies of Edna's admission and discharge cards, including my birth time, if I sent proof of my identity.

A month or so later I received information from the Royal Women's. My birth time was 3.18am.

My birth was recorded under the following heading: Still Births, Miscarriages, B.B.A., etc. Obviously it was not a miscarriage or stillbirth so it must have been B.B.A. whatever that meant.

Edna had almost died when I was born so perhaps B.B.A. was connected to a difficult birth. I racked my brains. Could B.B.A. stand for Breech Birth Assisted? It did.

No wonder Edna had almost died. A breech birth would be a horrendous ordeal. Her bad luck continued when she was compelled to place me for adoption two weeks later.

At this time I continued with my university studies and John worked part time for Tertiary and Further Education.

And then in 2002, during the June holidays, John and I flew to Britain for three weeks.

We had an overnighter in Singapore before a long arduous flight to London. The next day we joined a bus tour. Our itinerary took us through England, Wales, Scotland and Paris.

We soon settled back into our usual home life and I returned to my university studies and John to his part time work.

Tev invited us to an evening barbeque at his house. Alex, Tev's son, worked for the Endeavour Foundation and the occasion was in honour of his clients. We would meet Alex's wife, Aya, and young daughter, Sarah, and Tev's old friends, Errol and Liz.

It was the first social event I had enjoyed with Edna and I felt like Cinderella. Tev, who has an infectious laugh, laughed uproariously once he had consumed a few beers and it helped alleviate my nerves.

Could Edna relax and enjoy herself if she came to my house? I did not think so. She believed she had given away her rights when she relinquished me. The taboos were deeply embedded.

Towards the end of the year I invited Tev and Edna to spend Christmas Day with us. They declined. I think Edna was embarrassed to meet other members of my family such as my in-laws. She carried so much guilt and did not wish to be at the forefront of conversation.

That spring, Andrew asked us to lunch at Southbank, to meet his girlfriend Akiko. She was a charming Japanese girl with a great sense of humour. Lunch was a pleasant and light-hearted occasion.

At the end of the year Andrew finished his degree in a Bachelor of Information Technology (Computing Science) and began full time employment with Dialogue.

When adoption touches family, fallout is inevitable. During the forty years I spent as a wife and mother I noticed the effects in my own family. I know my husband John, and my oldest son, Chris, have each been affected.

When we met, John had no idea he would be involved in issues that plague an adoptee. He has become familiar with the psychological issues, the adoption triad and the highs and lows of searching for and reunion with birth family. Together we have experienced the excitement and joy when years of searching yielded successful results.

The fallout intensified after the first few years of our marriage because after my children were born I became obsessed with my lack of genetic information and grew more determined to find answers.

I was fortunate John was always empathetic. Apparently some spouses are not.

Chris, of my three sons, seemed most affected. He went silent if adoption was mentioned. I was mystified and eventually, I spoke to him about it. "Chris, I don't understand why you are so reticent to discuss adoption."

"Well, it's because I don't want you to be adopted," he said. "And I find it hard to come to terms with the fact that Granny and Grandpa aren't my biological grandparents."

I thought Chris had been in denial and I had taken his reticence as personal rejection. The fact that adoption affected my own children was a facet I had never previously considered.

I had known Edna for twenty years. Chris was thirty and it was high time he met his [birth] grandmother. He reacted negatively to my suggestion so once again I was confused and hurt. "Chris, why don't you want to meet Edna?"

"I don't want to be disloyal to Granny," Chris told me.

Disloyalty was certainly an issue of adoption. Adoptees were often accused of disloyalty towards their adoptive parents, if they searched for their birth families.

I assured Chris his feelings for Granny would not lessen if he met Edna. I explained that love had no limits. And, after all, Granny had been dead for nineteen years so she would not suffer. How mind-blowing that the guilt inherent in adoptive issues could affect the next generation so strongly.

Eventually Chris agreed to visit Edna and Tev. Kerryn, John and I would go too. I phoned Edna to arrange a time, but did not mention the fact Kerryn and Chris would accompany us. I thought she might renege, and I did not want to face that possibility.

Tev made afternoon tea and the visit went reasonably well considering Chris, Kerryn and Edna were complete strangers.

I always felt the loss of my biological family after such an event because it highlighted the fact that nothing could replace the lost years. That realisation always made me sad.

The following year I suggested Andrew meet Edna and he agreed. After a family discussion it was decided Chris and Kerryn would also accompany us. I phoned Edna to arrange a time but she was reluctant. She said she was not well enough to have visitors that day. Anyway she and Tev had planned to watch the cricket on television.

I was disappointed. I phoned my family and explained. They were disappointed too as they had psyched themselves up. Chris, Kerryn and Andrew knew the visit had been important to me so, to stave off despair, they suggested we meet at the Riverbend Café in Bulimba for a get together.

Consequently, due to our busy lives, Andrew never did meet Edna, and Chris and Kerryn never saw her again. Lachlan could not remember meeting her in his childhood. I had done as much as I could. Reunions with birth families can be tense and tenuous.

28

The Private Detective

The snow goose need not bathe to make itself white.
Neither need you do anything but be yourself.
– Lau Tzu

2003

I had explored every avenue to find Cyril Carlyle. He seemed to have vanished into thin air. The Salvation Army could not help me, but what about a private detective? Could we afford one? John and I, after much discussion, found Ivor in the Yellow Pages and made an appointment for the following week.

On the day, we arrived early into the city. We hurried up the street and soon located the address in a narrow three-storied building.

Apprehensively I pulled open a glass door and entered a small dark foyer. John and I perused the notice board and discovered Ivor's office was on the third floor. We clumped up a steep set of timber steps to an empty reception area and sat down awkwardly, filled with trepidation. Ten minutes later a tall middle-aged man with a serious expression emerged from one of the rooms. He wore a light toned check sports coat, white shirt, charcoal tie and grey trousers. His wavy salt and pepper hair and bushy white moustache suited his occupation perfectly. He invited us into his office and indicated where we should sit.

I explained my problem and handed over Cyril Carlyle's information. Ivor said he should be able to help me as he could access Medicare numbers, stressing that anyone living in Australia would have a Medicare card. He could also access driver's licences, and he had contacts at the Registrar General's Department if unexpected difficulties arose. He asked us to pay a set fee and advised us to contact him in six weeks.

I was assured by Ivor's confident manner, but nevertheless when I arrived home, I continued with my own searches.

Two days later I applied to the Registrar General's Department for the death certificate of John Carlyle, Cyril's father. I asked for a ten-year stretch from 1963 to 1972 inclusive.

Three weeks later I was informed no record of John Carlyle's death had been found during those years. I applied again for 1958 to 1962 inclusive.

Whilst waiting for news from our detective, John and I used the internet to trace two men connected with Edna.

In MyTrees.com we located Edwin McBroom, Edna's erstwhile husband. The result is as follows:

US Social Security Death Index [excerpt]

Name: Edwin McBroom

Birth Date: 9th August 1910

Date of Death: 26th January 1984

Residence (2/88 and prior): Louisiana

Last Residence (Zip): 71201 Monroe, Ouachita, L-A

Although Edna had last seen Edwin in 1943, it was now obvious he had not died during the war. He had survived until he was seventy-four years. Incredible!

And we discovered more information in a family history site. It seemed Edwin was the youngest of eight brothers and sisters, but the most astonishing information was the statement: 'Edwin had never married'. John and I were particularly amused because I have Edwin and Edna's marriage certificate. It was obvious he had never mentioned his Australian bride.

We also located Tev's birth father, Carl Winston Tevis, in the same site. The result is as follows:

US Social Security Death Index [excerpt]

Name: Carl W. Tevis

Birth Date: 12th August 1912

Date of Death: 28th July 1998

Residence (2/88 and Prior):

Last Residence (Zip): 85201 Mesa, Maricopa, AZ

Reliability of Data: Report verified with a family member on behalf of the family.

Carl Tevis had not died in the 1940s or 1950s but had lived until he was eighty-six years.

During childhood Tev was told his father was deceased. Now there was proof of another lie. Maybe Edna lied to allay any unwanted questions? If Tev had known his father was alive he may have been able to make contact. How unfair!

Apparently Carl Tevis asked Edna to join him in America after the war, but she declined.

In the meantime I also applied to the Registrar General's Department for the marriage certificate of John and Ethel Carlyle [Cyril's parents]. On the 7th March I received the following certificate:

Marriage Certificate [excerpt]

Names: John Carlyle and Ethel Mary Allardice

Date of Marriage: 27th December 1926.

Place of Marriage: St. Furban's Church, Ashgrove, according to the rights of the Roman Catholic Church.

Groom: John Carlyle

Occupation: Cabinetmaker

Age at Time of Marriage: 23 years

Birthplace: Brisbane

Parents: James Carlyle (Van Proprietor) and Bridget Scanlan

Bride: Ethel Mary

Occupation: Tailoress

Age at Time of Marriage: 19 years

Birthplace: Brisbane

Parents: Thomas Allardice (Railway Employee) and Lily McDonnell

At last the six-week wait was over and it was time to make contact with our detective. Understandably we were eager to hear his report.

John made the phone call early on Monday morning. Ivor answered his mobile in a brusque manner. Then he roused at John because his phone call was inconvenient as he had just arrived in the car park.

"Anyway you shouldn't have rung me," said Ivor.

"But you asked us to contact you after six weeks," protested John.

"No, I didn't," snapped Ivor. "I said I would ring you. I haven't anything to tell you yet. Don't call me. I'll call you." Then he switched off his phone.

Phew! Ivor was cranky in his old age. He had not given us any indication of how long the investigation would take. John and I would need every bit of patience we could muster.

A month passed then Ivor Moore phoned. He was in a good mood so I sighed with relief. He said he had changed tactics and would search for Cyril's sister, Alma Ethel. I was surprised because married women usually have a name change.

"Alma Ethel is an uncommon name," explained Ivor. "I've ignored her maiden name as she's probably married anyway, but I've located twelve Alma Ethel's living in Australia. We'll make inquiries, eliminate, and keep at it until we find the right one. I'll phone as soon as I have news."

I thanked Ivor and returned to my searches. Each new piece of family history data from the Registrar General's Department enabled me to move up to the next level.

Two weeks later Ivor phoned again and informed me he had eliminated ten Alma Ethels and would now investigate the two remaining women. One lived in Townsville and the other at Albany Creek.

"I've virtually ruled out Alma Ethel Brooks from Albany Creek," Ian explained. "I don't think she's the one. I'm going to concentrate on Alma Ethel Lawson in Townsville."

Why had Ivor eliminated Alma Ethel Brooks? Nevertheless, I was excited. The time was nigh.

During the following week I received three new certificates from the Registrar General's Department.

On the 2nd April, James and Bridget Carlyle's marriage certificate arrived [Cyril's grandparents]. It contained the following information:

Marriage Certificate [excerpt]

Names: James Carlyle and Bridget Scanlan

Date of Marriage: 7th January 1903

Place of Marriage: St. Patrick's Roman Catholic Church, Toowoomba

Groom: James Carlyle (Widower)

Birthplace: Avonbridge, Stirling, Scotland

Occupation: Van Proprietor

Age at Marriage: 36 years old

Parents: James Carlyle (Labourer) and Ann Turner

Bride: Bridget Scanlan

Birthplace: Glynn, Limerick, Ireland

Age at Marriage: 27 years old

Parents: John Scanlon (Farmer) and Mary Dalton

The second certificate was John Carlyle's birth certificate [Cyril's father]. It revealed the following information:

Birth Certificate [excerpt]

Name: John Carlyle

Birth Date: 7th November 1903

Place of Birth: Windsor Road, Redhill

Parents: James Carlyle (Van Proprietor) and Bridget Scanlan

The third certificate to arrive was John Carlyle's death certificate [Cyril's father]. It included the following information:

Death Certificate [excerpt]

Name: John Carlyle

Date of Death: 27th July 1962

Place of Death: Princess Alexandra Hospital South Brisbane

Age at Death: 58 years old

Reason for Death: Pneumonia, cerebral arteriosclerosis and an old cerebral haemorrhage

Certified in Writing by: A.E. Brooks, daughter, 35 Foster Street, Newmarket

Issue Living: Alma Ethel - 33 years

Issue Deceased: 1 male

John Carlyle had died in 1962 aged fifty-eight.

I examined his certificate meticulously and my eyes widened in astonishment when I spotted the person who had certified his death. It was none other than his daughter A. E. Brooks. Recorded under issue was: Alma Ethel 33 years.

So incredibly, John Carlyle's daughter, A.E. Brooks, was Alma Ethel Brooks, the woman from Albany Creek Ivor had eliminated.

Bingo! I had hit the jackpot and phoned Ivor. He was

pleased for me and would continue his inquiries.

Ivor contacted me a few days later with information on Alma Ethel Brooks. She owned a house in Albany Creek in partnership with a woman named Leanne.

"The fact Leanne and Alma are financially involved convinces me they are mother and daughter," explained Ivor. "This afternoon on the way home from work I'll go there and find out what I can."

"Will you speak to them?"

"No, I never barge straight in." He added, "I'll speak to the neighbours first and suss out the situation. I'll phone you tomorrow."

Tomorrow! Tomorrow I might know the answers. If Leanne was Alma's daughter she would be my [birth] first cousin.

Ivor phoned early the next afternoon. He had spoken to Alma's neighbours who said she no longer lived at Albany Creek. She moved into aged care because of a recent illness.

"Leanne is Alma's daughter and lives in the house with her husband and children. I have Leanne's phone numbers for you. It's up to you now."

I baulked at that. It would be another challenging phone call. I took down the numbers carefully, thanked Ivor for his work and hung up. I knew I needed to proceed, but would need to summon up lots of courage.

I shared my news with John and mentioned I was a little reticent to call Leanne. My story was quite outrageous because I did not have Cyril's name on my birth certificate.

During the next hour the usual butterflies bounced and fluttered in my stomach and produced a nauseous sensation. I dialled Leanne's landline but was disappointed when it rang out. I dialled her mobile number.

"Hello, Leanne speaking," said a woman with an affable manner.

"Hello, Leanne," I said. "My name is Jean Dowding. You don't know me, but I've been trying to locate Cyril Carlyle, a relative of yours."

"Yes, he's my uncle. I know all about him."

"Oh wonderful," I said. "I was adopted when I was a couple of weeks old and I'm pretty certain Cyril is my birth father. I've been searching for him for years. Recently I employed a private detective who found you and your mother."

"As I listened I just knew what you were going to say," said Leanne. "My mother's never mentioned this so maybe she didn't know anything. You know Cyril is dead don't you? He died in Sydney many years ago."

"Oh, that's so sad," I said. "I didn't know for sure, but I suspected something was wrong when we couldn't locate him."

"Mum lives in Mitchelton in an aged care complex now. She'll be very excited about you. Listen, I'd just walked into the bank when you rang and I have to go back to work soon. Let's make a time to talk tonight. You'll be a first cousin," added Leanne.

Leanne and I decided on 7.30pm. What a wonderful outcome. She sounded very warm and welcoming, and she was as excited as I was.

I phoned Leanne's landline right on time and divulged the absence of Cyril's name on my birth certificate. She was very understanding. I learnt she was thirty-nine years old and an only child and she had always lived with her mother. Her father had died when she was in her early twenties. Her husband's name was Brad and her daughters were Larissa and Carla. She worked as a receptionist in a doctor's surgery and was enthused about having a 'new' first cousin in her life.

"Do you know how Cyril died?"

"In a terrible accident that happened in 1951, when he was at work at the Hornsby Railway Station. The lines were supposed to be clear so he began to cross to the other platform when an unannounced train roared in. He squeezed under the lip of a platform and survived until the last carriage but regrettably it clipped him. He was severely injured and died later in the hospital."

Even though I had never met Cyril or seen a photo of him, a deep sense of sadness seeped through me. I imagined his terror as the train bore down on him.

"Oh how sad! What a horrible death. He was too young to die at twenty-three years."

"What year were you born?" asked Leanne.

"In 1948, three years before Cyril's death. I have his work record from Queensland Railways. He resigned in June 1949 and must have moved to Sydney. No wonder I couldn't find him."

Leanne had visited her mother late that afternoon.

"Mum was thrilled and wants to see you straight away. She said if you were a 'Carlyle', she'd know the moment she sees you. Your arrival is a wonderful surprise, but she knew nothing about your birth. She said she was only eighteen so no one would have mentioned it in those days. She said Cyril was a dark horse because she thought she knew everything about him."

"I'm happy she's pleased. I hope she won't be disappointed."

"I'm sure that won't be the case. Cyril married a Russian girl in Sydney in 1950 and they had a daughter named Maryanne. She was only six months old when he was killed. Years later, when I was about sixteen, Mum and I took a short holiday in Sydney and looked Maryanne up," said Leanne. "That's the only contact we've ever had with her and we've lost touch since. At the time I could see a definite family resemblance between us."

I was dumbfounded that I had had an unknown birth sister for fifty-two years. I vowed I would start to search for her as soon as possible. I marvelled at the remarkable events and people I had met since 1981 when I started searching. Now I had a birth sister. I could hardly believe it.

Maryanne had lost her father when she was only six months old and I felt sad for Cyril because he never knew either of his daughters.

My thoughts returned to my conversation with Leanne.

"What's Maryanne's married name?"

"I can't remember, but I'll ask Mum. At the time we saw her in Sydney she was divorced, and had a daughter called Danielle."

Leanne seemed to have an extroverted personality. She said her family would be away for the upcoming Easter holidays and she hoped to meet me beforehand. True to my introverted nature, I held back as I needed to draw breath.

Eventually I agreed to meet Leanne on Thursday after I attended a class at the Southbank Campus of Queensland College of Art. We would meet near the roundabout in Stanley Street, not far from the college and she would drive to Madonna Villa where we would meet her mother. I described the outfit I would wear and Leanne described her car, otherwise we may not have found each other.

On Thursday after my art class, I made my way to the designated meeting place. The city traffic was light on the fine autumn morning. I waited on the footpath in the dappled shade of a street tree and faced north, the direction from which Leanne would approach. I focused intently on every car as my excitement mounted.

Five minutes later I saw a dark green four-wheel drive roll slowly up to the roundabout. A young woman with short stylish blond hair and face make up was at the wheel. She spotted me and smiled and waved animatedly. I waved back to the woman who was clearly Leanne. She drove slowly around the roundabout and veered towards my side of the street. When she drew level with me she wound down the passenger window and leant across the seat.

"You're a Carlyle!' she shouted excitedly. "You look like Grandma Carlyle!"

Leanne was half Carlyle so she would know. She could not have said anything more appropriate and my smile was so wide I thought my face would split in two. An overwhelming sense of relief flooded through me. After years of research and innuendo I relaxed instantaneously. I could have given up so many times, but I had kept at it, and it had been worth it as I had found the other half of my birth family. What a significant moment!

As I stood on the curb with mounting excitement, I recalled the children's story "The Bunyip from Berkley's Creek": 'You're a bunyip,' called one bunyip to the other, 'you're just like me.'

When Leanne called out, "You're a Carlyle! You look like Grandma Carlyle!" I felt as happy as that bunyip. I felt I had finally come home.

Leanne parked the car and I hurried to the passenger door and opened it. As I leant in we clutched hands and smiled into each other's eyes. Leanne seemed very familiar as if I had always known her. Her golden hazel eyes were warm and her cheerful smile mirrored mine.

Leanne drove slowly along Stanley Street then braked at the first red light. At the same time she grabbed an A4 envelope from the parcel shelf and pushed it towards me.

"Here's your father," she said eagerly.

I thanked Leanne. What a surprise! I had searched for my birth father for so many years and now, unbelievably, I held his photograph in my hands?

"Open it and have a look," urged Leanne.

My hands shook as I bent back the flap and withdrew an A4 sized glossy colour print. I took a deep breath and turned it right side up.

In the photo Cyril, who was about nineteen or twenty, was dressed in a tan sports jacket with a white shirt and thin striped tie. His lips were curled in a small smile and his attractive brown eyes shone with a good-natured expression. He had clear skin, even features and small ears. His dark brown curly hair was cut short and brushed neatly to the side. I looked into his eyes and tears rolled down my cheeks. What a tragedy he had died at twenty-three.

"He's got my nose!" I squealed. "I have a photo taken at the same angle and my nose and top lip look similar. I would have been about his age too. There's also something about his smile that reminds me a bit of me."

I had seen a family likeness between Cyril and myself and it meant the world. I sat staring at the photo then thanked Leanne again.

"It's yours to keep," said Leanne.

On the way to Mitchelton Leanne diverted to Newmarket where our ancestors had owned acreage. James Carlyle, my [birth] paternal great grandfather, had run a carrier service. After James' death his wife, Bridget, sub-divided the land. Some of Bridget's family had built homes there and Leanne pointed out a few of the original houses.

Our Carlyle ancestors were of the Roman Catholic faith and had donated heavily to the building of St Ambrose Church at the bottom of the street.

James Carlyle had been born in Scotland, and Bridget, in Ireland. Another piece of the puzzle fell into place.

I was delighted to own some Scottish ancestry. I recalled how my adoptive mother spoke about her Scottish ancestors. And now, it had taken fifty-five years to prove that I did as well. My adoptive father's paternal ancestors were Scottish, as were my adoptive mother's maternal ancestors. The bagpipes had been revered in my childhood home and she had instructed Ian and I in Scottish customs and I was happy she had.

After a pleasant drive Leanne and I arrived at Madonna Villa and took the lift up to the second level. Alma had obviously been waiting and was in bed propped up with pillows. Leanne and I kissed her hello and she smiled a sweet smile as she welcomed us. Her eyes were hazel, her short, dark hair was wavy, and her skin fair. The nurses had applied makeup and dressed her in an attractive outfit.

Leanne had mentioned her mother's love of clothes and the particular care she took always took with her appearance. Alma's occupation had been as a tailoress, the same as her mother Ethel, my paternal [birth] grandmother, who had died at the age of twenty-six.

Leanne and Alma certainly knew how to put out the welcome mat. Alma said I was definitely a Carlyle and recognised a resemblance to Cyril. We were all keyed up, but as we did not want to tire Alma the visit soon came to an end. We kissed her goodbye then drove on to Leanne's house at Albany Creek where she planned to show me the family photo albums.

Leanne had a new eye-catching, well-maintained, two storeyed home, with a landscaped garden. The house contained a charming granny flat where Alma had lived before she suffered her stroke.

Leanne said she and her mother were annoyed with Edna's secrets and lies because otherwise we could have known each other twenty years ago.

"I wish you'd found us earlier as I'd love you to have known her before her stroke," said Leanne. "She's not the same person she used to be you know."

I told Leanne I wished the same thing and that I understood because the same fate had befallen my adoptive mother.

Leanne offered to lend me two large framed family portraits. One was Cyril and Alma as young children and the other, John and Ethel Carlyle, my paternal birth grandparents, on their wedding day.

My birth grandfather, John, who was always known as Jack, a cabinetmaker, had made the beautiful silky oak frame and mount for their wedding photograph.

Jack had worked for Trittons, a fine furniture store in the city. I was shown a photograph of a beautiful dining room suite he had made, now in storage in her attic. Some years later, Leanne would present me with an attractive silky oak coffee table that Jack had made. It has found a special place in my home and every time I see it I think of my paternal birth family.

Leanne and I perused the family albums and I noted with incredulity some likenesses between my paternal birth family and my sons. In his wedding photo Jack had a strong resemblance to Andrew, while in another photo his stance resembled Lachlan's. The shape of Christopher's face was reflected in Cyril's. Jack and Cyril had thick dark hair similar to Chris and Andrew. Many likenesses became apparent as I looked at more photographs. It was all such a new experience for me and once again I was becoming familiar with a family I never knew.

Leanne showed me photos of her mother as a young woman and was convinced she could see a family resemblance between Alma and myself. I noted Alma always wore a bracelet, something I have done for years. Leanne and I were also approximately the same height and we compared our hands and feet and noticed similarities. Apparently Alma and I had another similar habit: we always carried our lipsticks in our cleavage.

I was honoured Leanne offered to lend me the family portraits and albums; after all she had only met me that morning. She was an excellent person to divulge family stories as she and her mother had always been interested in family history.

I spied photos of Cyril as a young man and noted his legs were very similar to mine at the same age. Of course he had never grown old due to his premature death.

Leanne drove me back to my car at Southbank where we said goodbye and reassured each other we would get together again soon. When I arrived home I proudly hung the Carlyle family portraits.

During the next weeks I trawled through the Carlyle photo albums and made some photocopies. A month after the Easter holidays I spoke to Leanne on the phone and we arranged a time to return the portraits and albums. She invited John and me to her fortieth birthday party that many of my paternal birth relatives would be attending. John and I accepted with pleasure.

Eventually, I learnt my birth sister's married name was Maryanne Pender, and it was not long before John and I checked electoral rolls and white pages etcetera for Sydney and New South Wales, but we had no luck.

I applied for two more certificates, this time, from the New South Wales Registrar General's Department. The first was Cyril's death certificate and contained the following information:

Death Certificate [excerpt]

Name: Cyril John Carlyle

Date of Death: 27th April 1951

Age at Death: 23 years

Place of Death: Hornsby District Hospital, New South Wales

Cause of Death: Shock and injuries accidentally received whilst crossing a railway line in performance of his duty and being struck by a train and knocked to the permanent way

Occupation Rank or Profession: Railway Porter

Wife: Katharyna Carlyle nee Welichko

Issue: Mary A. six months

Mother: Ethel Carlyle nee Allardice (deceased)

Father: John Joseph Carlyle

Buried on the thirtieth April 1951, in Catholic Cemetery, Northern Suburbs Sydney.

The second was Cyril's marriage certificate and contained the following information:

Marriage Certificate [excerpt]

Names: Cyril John Carlyle and Katharyna Welichko

Date of Marriage: 29th March 1950

Place of Marriage: Registrar General's Office, Sydney

Groom: Cyril John Carlyle

Age at Marriage: Twenty-two years

Birthplace: Brisbane, Queensland

Usual Occupation: Railway Porter

Parents: John Joseph Carlyle (cabinet maker) and Ethel Mary Carlyle nee Allardice (deceased)

Bride: Katharyna Welichko

Age at Marriage: Twenty-five years

Birthplace: Tschernigow, Ukraine, United Soviet States of Russia

Usual Occupation: Domestic

Parents: Gregory Welichko (labourer) and Maria Meshkowa

On Cyril's death certificate I noted the correct spelling of my birth sister's first name. It was Mary not Maryanne. Mary's maiden name had been Mary A. Carlyle. The A. was obviously Ann or Anne.

By now I had accumulated a mammoth amount of paper work that related to my adoption and family research. During the next week I organised everything into ring binders.

A few weeks later I returned to my search for my birth sister Mary, but came up with nothing.

I considered contacting the Salvation Army again. In the past they would not search for Cyril and it was after that setback I had employed the detective.

Another week passed before I wrote to the Salvation Army and asked them to locate my birth sister. I explained the assignation between Cyril and Edna and sent photos of the three of us and Cyril's birth, death, and marriage certificates. I was optimistic the Salvation Army investigators might come to a positive decision based on likenesses between us.

Then on the 1st May, a Salvation Army officer contacted me and offered to search for Mary. I was thrilled. I would be required to pay a small fee up front and perhaps more for searches as the investigation proceeded. The officer would be in touch as soon as she had news.

John and I attended my birth cousin Leanne's fortieth birthday party where everyone wore fancy dress and that produced much hilarity. I met her family, her friends, and a number of other paternal birth cousins. I spent some time with my paternal birth aunt Alma. It was one of the many times our families would get together.

Someone asked me whether Cyril's name was on my birth certificate. I found it a complex situation to be in. Leanne had confessed that a few of her friends had warned her to be a bit wary of me when I turned up out of the blue. "What does she want?" was a catch cry. I am happy to say Leanne did not doubt my authenticity for a minute.

Not long after I found my paternal birth family I had considered taking a DNA test. I contacted a suitable laboratory and was informed if the test were taken with relatives, who were biologically removed, such as a half-sister, first cousin or aunt, the result might be inconclusive. It was also very expensive. I decided to shelve that idea for the moment.

Although I was convinced I was Cyril's birth daughter, the fact his name was not on my birth certificate created much insecurity within me. If only Edna had divulged my father's name I would have been spared a lot of pain.

At this time, I also finished my degree in a Bachelor of Fine Art. On 13th September 2003 I attended the official Griffith University ceremony where I proudly took the prized document in my hands.

I had majored with a credit in painting, my artwork being mostly conceptual because I had plugged in to my painful experiences as an adoptee and transferred that to canvas and other media. My technique could have used refinement, but at least I had the passion to imbue my work with emotive content.

The search for my birth sister, Mary, continued. In October, the Salvation Army contacted me and requested an extra fee for further investigations. They had progressed to the point where contact with Mary might be possible before Christmas, and were thrilled it might be an early Christmas present for me and sent me the following letter:

The Salvation Army

Date 25/11/2003

Dear Mrs Dowding,

Re: Pender, Mary A. (probably Ann)

Quote Ref No. Qld08383

The Salvation Army Family Tracing Service is endeavouring to locate your half-sister on your behalf. New South Wales has been able to conduct searches, which have offered the following information:

Your sister was born Mary Ann Carlyle on 24th October 1950. Her parents are recorded as Cyril John Carlyle and Katherina Carlyle (nee Welichko).

This information was obtained through extra searches costing $50.00. Can you offer to pay the extra fee by making a cheque or money order out to The Salvation Army Family Tracing Service, Sydney for $50.00, please and thank you?

We can encourage you by saying that with this information and also some information from searches, we now have further access to search options.

We pray and hope Mary can be located. When we have news, we will certainly be in contact.

Awaiting your reply,

May God bless you.

Yours sincerely,

DIRECTOR FAMILY TRACING SERVICE

Early in December I received exciting news. Mary had been found so I was overjoyed. The search had not been easy as Mary's married name turned out to be Binder not Pender, so no wonder she had been elusive. The investigators had resorted to searches in the Registrar General's Department and had done a wonderful job.

The Salvation Army had passed on my name, address and photos to Mary and now it was her decision whether to contact me or not. I was the 'searcher' so I was not given Mary's particulars and she, as the 'found' person, had the option to remain hidden.

The Salvation Army officer shared in my happiness and was of the opinion Mary would definitely be in touch because, in their experience, people were usually flattered to have someone search for them. Once again I would play the waiting game so prevalent in my journey of search and reunion.

A few weeks later I received the following letter from the Salvation Army.

Date 19/12/2003

Dear Jean,

What wonderful news for you! May it not be too long before Mary has made contact with us again.

Thank you for the information of your change of address details for February next year. May you enjoy a very happy Christmas.

We will be in contact as soon as we hear. If Mary chooses to contact you direct, we would love to share in it with you.

May God bless you.

Yours sincerely,

DIRECTOR FAMILY TRACING SERVICE

Christmas was close. One afternoon I arrived home to find John in a highly stressed state.

"What's wrong?" I asked.

"I'm so sorry!" said John. "You won't believe what I've done. Mary left a message with her phone number on our answering machine, and I deleted it by mistake."

"Oh no!" My shoulders slumped. "You mean you deleted the message before you took down the number?"

"Yes, I'm so sorry," said a penitent John.

I would have loved to hear Mary's voice. I now had no way of contacting her. John's expression was painful. He looked so discouraged. I think he was more upset than I was. Suddenly I said, "I'll phone the Salvation Army and ask them to contact Mary again. I'm sure they won't mind."

The Salvation Army officer assured me it was no trouble and later that day she phoned. Mary knew about the deleted message and would contact me soon. What a relief! I played the waiting game again.

One day I arrived home and found Mary had left another message on our answering machine. Her voice was low pitched and pleasant and she exuded a quiet confidence as she invited me to call her back anytime. I copied down her number with care.

I was aware of a lump in my throat and accelerated heart rate as I dialled Mary's number. She answered on the third ring. We chattered amicably for some time and I came to the conclusion that her personality was introverted and she seemed a bit reluctant to jump into a relationship too quickly.

Mary said she had another half-sister, who was older than she, named Cecelia. She stressed she was not used to large families and did not feel she could start now. After the death of her father, Cyril, in 1951, her mother, Cecelia, and she had moved in with her grandparents. They were Russian immigrants with a language barrier and had not socialised much if at all. Consequently, she was used to a small family and quiet life.

"My husband and I were divorced many years ago," she said. "After that I became a teacher then completed a university degree. At the moment I work for the Education Department as the Senior Education officer in Communications and Translation."

Mary lives in St Peters, a Sydney suburb, and was renovating her terrace house. Her daughter, Danielle, now married lives in Melbourne, so Mary lived with her dogs, Sonsa and Malchyk. Mary and I spent time discussing our dogs because, for us, they were common ground.

"What was your first job?" I then asked.

"I worked for the Registrar General's Department of Births, Deaths and Marriages," said Mary.

I almost laughed. During my onerous search I had been in contact with the Registrar General's Department for more than twenty years and applied for numerous certificates.

My thoughts returned to the present moment and I listened to Mary share more of her life.

Her mother, sister and she had continued to live with her grandparents for many years. Their lives had not been easy as her mother, now deceased, had developed schizophrenia and was hospitalised countless times. During her mother's hospitalisation she had received numerous horrific shock treatments and I could feel Mary's pain as she revived those unhappy memories.

Mary had no memory of her father, Cyril, and knew little about him. She knew even less about her paternal ancestors, the Carlyles, although she had met Alma and Leanne once.

"I wouldn't expect you to meet everyone in my family immediately. Perhaps never! Maybe just you and I should meet," I suggested. "We'll take it slow and get to know each other first."

"I don't feel that way about you. I'd like to meet you as you took the trouble to find me. But I don't want to be involved in a big family because I'm just not used to it. Anyway, my mother was always a bit hurt about the lack of contact from my father's family after his death. I feel it's too late to start now," added Mary.

I was aware Mary had suffered deprivation due to her lack of paternal knowledge. It is a strange coincidence that my other birth sibling, Tev, had also suffered the same deprivation.

I had read that ignorance about one parent can affect mental health and lead to feelings of insecurity in an affected individual. An adoptee that has no knowledge of either parent may end up in a lifetime search for her unknown parentage. I should know.

Mary and I shared some information about our parents. I discussed the relationship between Edna and Cyril and mentioned their visit to the theatre in 1947. Mary, who did have minor knowledge of her father, gleaned from her mother, shared it with me.

"Yes, that sounds right," said Mary. "Mum said he loved the theatre. He also liked a tipple."

"I understand his father, Jack, was a heavy drinker," I added.

As our conversation came to an end Mary and I decided we would email photos soon.

Would Mary and I ever meet? During the next months we emailed lots of messages and photos to each other and compared likenesses. Two photos of us from the past, in above the knee dresses, showed almost identically shaped knees and legs. I was three inches taller than Mary at five feet seven inches. Her eyes were brown and we both had dark curly hair in early life. I noted a likeness to Cyril around her eyes when she smiled. Getting to know each other via email was not ideal, but we managed.

Around this time, John and I decided to sell our home at Orchard Beach and move to Warwick. We had often yearned for more land since we had sold our farm, so we purchased five hundred and sixty acres on the Cunningham Highway, south of Warwick. Our new property was known as The Glen. We would live in an historical house that included a large garden with hundreds of roses.

During the coming weeks John and I began to pack up our belongings and clean our house rigorously for the real estate market.

Cyril (Carolann's birth father) in the 1940s.

Carolann, her adoptive mother, Mary, and pet, Kim, in 1968.
Photographer: Jack Gordon.

Carolann and John on one of their first dates at the Festival hall in Brisbane in 1967. Stirling Studios.

Carolann and John at Cloudland Brisbane in 1968. Cloudland Photographer.

Edna (Carolann's birth mother) aged twenty-eight at Coolum Beach in 1944. Photographer: Carl Tevis.

Carolann aged thirty-three in 1981 holding Andrew, with Chris in the centre and Lachlan on the right. Photographer: John Dowding.

Carolann in 1968 wearing a suit made by her adoptive mother, Mary. Photographer: Geoff Pike.

Edna (Carolann's birth mother) with her son Tev in the 1950s.

Carolann in 1968 wearing a ball gown sewn by her adoptive mother, Mary. Photographer: Bobby Gordon.

Edna (Carolann's birth mother) in 1949. Photographer: family member.

Carolann aged twenty-six with her son Chris at Byron Bay in 1974.
Photographer: John Dowding.

Edna (Carolann's birth mother) aged twenty-seven
at Coolum Beach in 1944. Photographer: Carl Tevis.

John and Carolann in May 1969. Selwyn Studios.

Jack and Mary (Carolann's adoptive parents in 1969. Selwyn Studios.

Carolann with her adoptive mother, Mary, in 1978.
Photographer: John Dowding.

29

Final Goodbye

The journey of a thousand miles begins with one step.
– Lau Tzu

2004

In the New Year, John and I continued packing for the move to Warwick, which was in a few weeks.

Late in January we visited Edna and Tev. In a few months they would move to north Queensland where, Tev's son, Alex was a detective in the Cairns police force.

John and I had acquired a cute grey miniature poodle named Louis, and since Tev and Edna were dog lovers, we took Louis with us. When Edna saw Louis for the first time, she scoffed at me for owning a poodle. She seemed to believe that only the bourgeois would own a poodle.

Later that afternoon John and I said goodbye to Tev and Edna. As I led Louis towards our vehicle Edna looked down at him and smiled.

"He is a nice little dog," she said. Edna had recovered from her resistance to him.

I had noticed, on occasion, Edna displayed some negative attitudes towards me. I deduced this was about my higher socio economic circumstances, and I found this problematic as I sought her acceptance.

I am the product of nature [birth family] and nurture [adoptive family]. My socio-economic circumstances are what they are because Edna relinquished me. I should not be blamed. I expected more understanding and maturity from Edna but I also believed she was embarrassed and insecure by believing herself to be in a lower socio economic situation.

In February, John and I moved to our new property. Our house in Orchard Beach, as yet unsold, was left in the capable hands of our real estate agent.

My birth cousin, Leanne, and her family visited us at The Glen on several occasions. On one occasion she brought her mother, Alma, for a one-off visit. It was not an easy task because Alma was paralysed on one side and wheelchair bound. Nevertheless, we enjoyed a very special day.

In April, John and I received a phone call from Edna and Tev just before they moved to North Queensland. Although I did not know it at the time, it was a good bye. I would never see Edna again.

I heard more about Jack Carlyle, my paternal grandfather, from Leanne. He led a rather sad existence that began in 1933 with the death of his twenty–six year old wife.

Ethel Mary, my paternal grandmother, burnt her arm and leg during an accident with a petrol iron. Soon the burns turned septic and then things went from bad to worse. In the end she was hospitalised with septicaemia. Her condition worsened and soon became septic pneumonia. Antibiotics were not available in 1933 and tragically she died from heart failure.

At the time, she was pregnant with her third child. Her children, Cyril, six and Alma four, were left motherless.

Her husband, Jack, was devastated. His mother-in-law, never his greatest fan, exacerbated his distress when she lashed out and accused him of murder.

An inquest was held into Ethel's death and family members made tough court appearances. Ultimately, much to everyone's relief, her death was declared accidental.

Jack's mother-in-law rejected him and her grandchildren, so the two families were estranged. He was overloaded with grief, a full-time job and care of his two young children. Regrettably he suffered a nervous breakdown.

The extended Carlyle family stepped in to help. Jack's mother, Bridget, lived nearby and his sister, Mary, who was childless, cared for Cyril and Alma.

Jack either resigned from, or lost his job with Trittons. When he recovered he started a job with Queensland Railways in Ipswich.

Cyril attended state school in Ipswich and later Ipswich Grammar School. Alma attended St Ambrose's at Newmarket and later St Mary's Convent in Ipswich.

One day John and I visited the archives and obtained a copy of the inquest into Ethel's death.

For many years Jack Carlyle continued to mourn his wife Ethel. He had always been a drinker but, after his wife's death, he became a heavy drinker. And every year on the anniversary of her death he succumbed to an alcohol-induced bender that lasted a few weeks.

Back in 1951 when my birth father, Cyril, died accidently at the age of twenty-three, Jack was distraught. Cyril and his father, Jack, had a close relationship. It was the second loss he had endured in seventeen years. Every year, on the anniversary of his son's death, he succumbed to another alcohol-induced bender.

Back in 1982, Edna said, my birth father had died of a cerebral haemorrhage while working on the railway lines and afterwards she received a nasty letter from his parents blaming her for his death. Recently I have compared Edna's tale with the facts of Cyril's death and I am convinced Cyril's father, Jack Carlyle, wrote that nasty letter to Edna in 1951. Perhaps Jack harassed her in other ways with phone calls or visits when he was intoxicated on future anniversaries of Cyril's death. It was understandable he knew her whereabouts as they both worked for Queensland Railways.

It was wrong of Jack to blame Edna. Unfortunately in his anguish he had needed to vent and he fanned the flames of his despair with alcohol.

In 1948, Cyril and Jack may have disagreed with my relinquishment and resentment between Edna and the Carlyles began at that time. Jack and Cyril have now passed away so I will never have the opportunity to hear their side.

Leanne said the Carlyles were very family oriented so she believes Cyril and Jack wanted me. They may have demanded Edna tell them who had adopted me. Perhaps she told them I had died.

Cyril attempted to have involvement in my life when he wrote to the authorities claiming paternity in 1948, but eventually I was lost to adoption so perhaps he was heartbroken. In view of the hopeless situation, it made sense that he resigned from Queensland Railways in 1949 and moved to Sydney to start a new life.

Why did Edna refuse to tell me my birth father's name if he was deceased? She said 'it' might start up again if she told me his name. I can only assume 'it' meant the harassment she suffered at the hands of an intoxicated Jack Carlyle on the anniversaries of Cyril's death.

In 1982, when we first contacted Edna, Jack Carlyle would have been seventy-eight years old if he was alive. Edna probably feared he was. Her fear was well founded because I would have contacted the Carlyles as soon as I knew they were my birth relatives.

It has taken me years to collect enough information to assemble the jigsaw of my past, but at last I have come up with a possible explanation.

In 1948, Edna told June and Doctor Fielding I was legitimate and we all know that was a downright lie. Then, in 1982, she explained her plan to me.

"If I'd kept you I would've given you the surname McBroom, just as I did for Tevy."

Edna seemed ashamed to be the mother of illegitimate children and in 1940s who can blame her? Unmarried mothers were ostracised. She wished to be seen as a respectable married woman and she made sure Tev was protected from the disgrace of illegitimacy by bestowing the name McBroom on him. If Tev and I had our birth fathers names on our birth certificates, respectability would have been impossible.

In 1947, Queensland Railways officially classed Edna

as a deserted wife with one child. Her job may have been in jeopardy when she became pregnant for the second time. It might explain her obsession to keep my birth a secret.

Would Queensland Railways have sacked her in 1947? It was certainly possible. In 1970, my friend, Anna, a married woman and librarian for the Warwick City Council, was sacked immediately when her employers discovered she was pregnant.

Edna relinquished me because of poverty. Today, she would have no need to relinquish me. She would be classed as a single mother with two children. Society would accept her situation and she would be entitled to a supporting mother's benefit.

Edna (Carolann's birth mother)
aged twenty-one in 1938.

30

Two Family Occasions

And the day came when the risk to remain tight in a bud
was more painful than the risk it took to blossom.
– Anaïs Nin

2004

Andrew and his fiancée, Akiko, surprised us with an announcement. Akiko's study visa was due to run out. They did not wish to be separated so they would marry in April and then she would apply for permanent residency.

On the morning of the wedding John and I arrived at the Brisbane Registry Office with only minutes to spare. We had driven from Warwick, but because of a landslide at Cunningham's Gap we had taken the longer route via Toowoomba.

We hurried into the chapel where Chris, Kerryn, Lachlan and Jo were already seated. Andrew and Akiko, the smartly attired bride and groom, stood at the front, ready to start. The ceremony proceeded smoothly and later that day our party of eight had a celebration in the Little Tokyo Restaurant where we partook of delectable cuisine and hot sake.

On a spring afternoon in October 2005, Andrew and Akiko, in full wedding regalia married in the landscaped grounds of the Sirromet Winery at Mount Cotton. A personable female celebrant conducted the reaffirmation of vows.

Akiko's parents, brother, and a friend of the family had travelled from Japan for the occasion and the bride and groom brimmed with happiness.

Akiko looked gorgeous in a full-length, off the shoulder, satin gown that contrasted beautifully with her dark hair and eyes. She had delicate flowers, artistically placed in her upswept hair, overlaid with a transparent veil. Andrew looked handsome in his black pin striped suit with blue accessories that offset his thick dark hair and grey eyes and accentuated his height of over six foot two inches.

In May, 2006, John and I sold The Glen and moved back to the Redlands, into an almost new ranch style house, on a small acreage at Thornlands.

31

The Mediterranean

Whatever you do may seem insignificant to you,
but it is most important that you do it.
– Mohandas Gandhi

2006

John and I were invited to a sixtieth birthday party on a small island in the Mediterranean. We accepted the invitation and proceeded to make arrangements.

My friend Marilena, through mitigating circumstances, had only one biological relative from Australia to attend her party in Lipari. She invited a group of Australian friends who would make up for the absence of family.

As an adoptee, I have always been very aware I was not biologically connected to the people I called mother, father, brother, and cousins. The adoption experience altered the attitude many have that only biological relatives can be close family members. I had to believe in that, otherwise, I felt my whole life was a sham.

John and I, and Marilena's other friends became her family on the island of Lipari and were treated as such by her. As an adoptee, I believe that non-biologically related people can, in fact, be as close to each other as biologically related relatives.

In August we flew to Italy via Korea. We arrived at the Italian airport at dusk and boarded a mini bus, with other passengers, for the journey into Rome.

An enthusiastic Italian driver threw our luggage into the back of his vehicle, jumped in and revved up the engine. He proceeded to drive at breakneck speed while we clung to our seats. I lost all sense of direction as the little bus careened and bumped its way through the many twists and turns on the dark country road.

We rolled our eyes at each other as we swerved from side to side throughout the entire trip. Everyone, maybe even the driver, was astonished when we pulled up outside the Cicerone Hotel in Rome, still in one piece. Our luggage was ejected hurriedly amid much laughter and friendly talk in broken English.

The following night John and I joined a welcome dinner for our bus tour that would begin early the next morning and continue for fifteen days.

We toured Italy, as far north as Venice, and Sicily, as far south as Palermo. We also visited the Vatican, Florence, the beguiling ancient hill town of Assisi, the dazzling isle of Capri, Sorrento, Naples and many churches and monasteries. A highlight of our tour was a moonlight dinner-cruise around the island of Venice.

Naples was our last port of call before our voyage across the Mediterranean to Sicily. In the early evening our bus boarded a huge car ferry, while we, and our tour group, made our way to our cabins. John and I slept well and woke just in time to see the sun rise over Sicily. We rejoined the bus and later that day settled into a Sicilian hotel where we were based for two days. Eventually we continued our tour of Sicily visiting Taormina, Agrigento, and Mt Etna.

Our tour ended in the Sicilian city of Palermo, where John and I stayed for two more nights before we boarded a small ferry for the island of Lipari where the sixtieth birthday party was to be held.

Lipari was three hours by sea and the ferry stopped at many small islands on the way. Notices and rules were posted in Italian and the captain and crew spoke little English.

An hour into the voyage we purchased a cup of strong black coffee in miniscule cups. When we inquired about milk and sugar, we were given the message they were absolute no-nos.

We were quite anxious during the voyage because we had no idea where we were, and feared we would disembark at the wrong island, the fate of two German backpackers who just managed to scramble back on board.

Halfway through the journey we were informed, in broken English, we would reach Lipari about 6.00pm.

The sea was mirror calm and a fabulous blue. I was fascinated when volcanos, such as Stromboli, rose unexpectedly from the depths. On closer inspection I could pick out tiny farms and cottages dotted about the barren cliffs. John and I wondered how the farmers could successfully produce food from such an environment.

Our ferry finally reached Lipari at dusk where we were startled to see a city sparkling with lights. The streets were busy and full of noisy cars and scooters. Lipari certainly did not resemble a desert island. I noted a variety of shops, restaurants, wharfs and historic buildings. We caught a taxi to our hotel where, surprisingly, the receptionist was a young Australian woman, married to a Liparian.

The next day we met up with our friend from Brisbane, Marilena. Her birth had taken place on the island, sixty years ago, and she was there to celebrate in the old villa where she was born.

Casa di Mandorla, House of Almonds, was still owned by Marilena's relatives. It exuded an appealing Mediterranean aura with its smooth stonewalls and bright blue trims. The building, like many other villas, clung to the edge of the cliffs and overlooked the sea. At night, in the full moon, it was exquisite. In front of the villa a garden sloped down the cliffs, where an assortment of plants grew, including an almond tree, herbs, and Marilena's favourite, the Italian delicacy, Prickly Pear.

On one occasion, we accompanied Marilena and other guests down a steep path to swim in the pristine waters. The seabed is comprised of rock, not mud or sand, a fact that accounts for the pure condition of the water. The beach was covered in sharp black stones so we wore our shoes to the water's edge.

The colour of the sea reminded me of the 'blue bags' my mother added to her white washing when I was a child. Our Australian seas, by contrast, have a definite greenish cast.

On the day of the party, all Marilena's guests gathered on the patio to enjoy the fine weather and magnificent view. The celebratory food appeared and the drink flowed.

Marilena's aunt, who lived on Lipari and spoke little English, made the pasta sauce then Marilena boiled the pasta. When the sauce was heated a half a cup of extra olive oil was added, which seemed excessive, but it tasted fine.

John cooked Italian sausages on the barbeque and added them to the many cheeses and breads that were part of the feast. Dessert was a huge Italian style cake, always part of festive occasions for the Italian family.

I found a moment to myself and stood at the edge of the patio and gazed at the Mediterranean vista. I reflected on my adoptive and birth families, and how far away they were from the little island. I had also come far on my adoptive journey and was thrilled I no longer lived with an empty past, although it had taken courage, persistence and time to arrive at that point.

But I realised, good friends were precious too and they would care about me even if I had never started my journey. I moved away from the edge of the patio and rejoined the party.

After five days of excitement on Lipari, John and I boarded the little ferry for the uneventful return voyage to Palermo. We spent another two nights in the Palermo hotel then caught an inter-country flight back to Rome. Later that day we boarded a Korean airliner, for a two-night stopover in South Korea, before we continued on to Australia.

Back home I received sad news. Tev phoned and informed me Edna had passed away. She was eighty-nine years old. She had lived a long life despite a number of heart attacks and other various health issues.

Tev cared for Edna at home for as long as he could, but during the last year of Edna's life she had stayed in an aged care facility in Innisfail. I had recently organised the facility's phone number and intended to phone her in the next week or so but I missed her.

She had been part of my life for twenty-five years and died too young, regardless of her age, as she and I needed more time to catch up on the lost years. Edna was cremated in a private ceremony at the crematorium chapel in Innisfail. John and I did not attend.

My relationship with Edna was dissimilar to the one I had with my adoptive mother, Mary. Edna was never 'there' for me as my adoptive mother had been. I spent my childhood with my adoptive mother and that created a bond I could not form with Edna. My adoptive mother had been a loving grandmother to my children. Edna hardly knew them.

Nevertheless, Edna and I were genetically mother and daughter and nothing could alter that bond.

In 2008, I applied to the Registrar of Births, Deaths and Marriages for Edna's death certificate. I included numerous identification documents to prove I was her birth daughter.

Some weeks later I was staggered when I received a phone call from that department. The officer explained I was not entitled to Edna's death certificate because, due to my adoption, my name did not appear on Edna's certificate.

Tev was the only recorded offspring. The department knew I was Edna's birth daughter, but that did not equate entitlement. The officer explained Tev's rights [not mine as an adoptee] came first. He might not know I existed. Of course I told her he did know, but that made little difference.

The officer suggested I ask Tev's permission then they would comply if they received a signed statement from him.

Once again I was astounded by the restraints placed on adoptees. I felt the usual anger and frustration build inside me.

A few days later I wrote to Tev, explained and included a cheque, the correct form, and a drafted letter for him to sign. He was happy to help.

The record of an adoptee's birth is scratched from their birth parents' certificates to be included on their adoptive parents' certificates. My adoptive parents appeared to have given birth to me in the usual way.

According to Edna's death certificate, she had given birth to only one child.

I received Edna's death certificate in the mail a few weeks later. It contained the following information:

Death Certificate [excerpt]

Name: Edna Doris McBroom

Date of Death: 1st March 2007

Place of Death: Innisfail Hospital, Innisfail

Age at Death: 89 years, a widow

Married to Whom: Edwin McBroom in 1942

Occupation: Railway Employee

Born: Tivoli, Queensland

Father: Frederick Fechner

Mother: Martha Henrietta Fechner/Bell (nee Siemsen)

Issue Living: William C.

Cause of Death: 1. (a) Ventricular arrhythmia (b) Ischemic Cardiovascular disease 2. Chronic renal failure, hypertension.

I added Edna's death certificate to my family history folder.

32

The Birthday Gift

No one saves us but ourselves. No one can
and no one may. We ourselves must walk
the path.
– Buddha

2007

On January 18th John presented me with a thoughtful birthday gift. It was a return airline ticket to Sydney for us both. The reason was to meet Mary, my birth sister. I was surprised when I learnt John and Mary had prearranged a suitable date.

It was a fantastic present and I was appreciative of his kind-heartedness, but as the day drew closer the usual butterflies flitted frantically and created a nauseous feeling. I knew I would be challenged.

Mary and I spoke on the phone just before the big day and we admitted we were nervous. She confessed she would have preferred our initial meeting to be one on one, but she was so impressed with John's gift she consented to his being present.

On the day of our flight John and I rose in the dark. The ungodly hour was due to daylight saving in New South Wales. We were to meet Mary at midday on the steps of the Sydney Opera House. Our flight was uneventful and we arrived early at Circular Quay, explored The Rocks area then strolled along the promenade to view Sydney's radiant harbour.

At 11.30am we made our way to the Opera House and chose a position in the middle of the bottom step. My hands were shaking and my heart beat fast as I scrutinised the passersby.

On the dot of midday I noticed a woman with short blond hair walk slowly towards us. She wore an attractive dusky pink lace top and black slacks and shoes. She looked around nervously. I had seen photos of Mary and, although a photo is no substitute for real life, I felt sure the woman was she. I gave a little wave and she lifted her hand in acknowledgement and walked towards us. John and I stood up and met her halfway. I do not recall our introductions because the occasion was another of those strange, nervous moments when one meets a close relative late in life. Mary was fifty-seven years old and I was fifty-nine.

Mary, John and I discussed lunch as we strolled back along the promenade. We chose a restaurant and took a table on the terrace with an impressive harbour view. We thoroughly enjoyed each other's company and the delicious food and wine. I am sure we were all very relieved our conversation flowed freely.

"I'm surprised at how well this reunion went," admitted Mary in the middle of lunch. "It hasn't been half as bad as I thought it would be."

After a leisurely lunch Mary, John and I walked back to Circular Quay and caught the train to St Peters Station. From there it was just a short walk to Mary's terrace house. We were fascinated to see inside an original for the first time.

After Mary's dogs got over their excitement we were introduced. We met Sonsa ['Sunshine' in Russian] and Malchyk ['Boy' in Russian]. Mary served afternoon tea and we relaxed in her courtyard. We found time to examine photos of my recent reunion with our paternal relatives, the Carlyles, and some of Mary's Russian family. Late in the afternoon, Mary drove us to the airport and we said our goodbyes.

It was evening when we arrived home after a smooth and uneventful flight. At bedtime, my mind whirled with thoughts of the day and I found it difficult to sleep. Mary and I had introverted personalities and being a little reticent may have put off meeting for a long time, if John had not intervened. What a memorable day it had been.

During the following weeks I had some misgivings and suffered the usual fears of rejection. What had Mary thought of me? Would she wish to carry on a relationship?

Over time it was clear that I need not have worried as we kept in touch.

John and I sold our property at Thornlands and moved back to Redland Bay in June 2007, into a twelve-year-old house with a splendid bay view.

During the coming months we proceeded to carry out decorating and landscaping. The view was similar to that of my childhood. We enjoyed the passing marine traffic, particularly the ferries and barges that plied passengers and vehicles to the bay islands.

I enjoyed the many moods of the sea, the boats lying at anchor, the distant islands, the rustle of easterly breezes in the gum trees, and the cry of sea birds brought back memories of my childhood.

Mary (Carolann's birth sister) and husband in 1970. Paramount Studios.

33

Change of Name

One of my rules is: Never try to do anything.
Just do it.
– Ani Defranco

2007

I applied to change my name, from Jean Isobel Dowding to Carolann Carlyle Dowding in September. I received my change of name certificate from the Registrar General's Department on 16th October.

Carol Ann McBroom was my original birth name. I linked Carol and Ann together to form a new Christian name because I needed to differentiate from John's sister, Carol, and my mother in law, Caroline. Then I added my birth father's surname, Carlyle, as my middle name.

Changing one's name creates mountains of paper work and fuss. I changed all my cards, driver's licence and passport. I informed dentists, doctors and others.

I was stunned at the positive attention I received. Many people showed interest in my reasons and complimented my name choice.

Working through the arduous process of change caused me to reflect and delve deeper into the negative psychological aspects of adoption.

One of the worst issues I (and other adoptees) faced at the time of adoption was the elimination of my identity. Added to that, I was disgruntled with authorities who locked up my personal information, then dished it out, as they saw fit. Some personal information may be hidden forever.

Names are important. Today, in an overseas adoption, adoptive parents are encouraged to retain the adoptees original first name to help preserve the adoptee's lost culture. If the adoptee is over twelve years their original birth name must be retained unless their name happens to mean something derogatory in English.

During adoptee related workshops, I was encouraged to increase my 'sense of self' and I believe this happened during my name change.

I did not ask to be separated from my biological family and I had no say when my identity was altered. My name change makes a statement about that lost identity.

Most non-adoptees would not give a moment's thought to the atrociousness of having one's identity altered and hidden. They do not consider the power and control issues that are involved. Because of those issues adoptees often feel powerless so I regained some of that lost power when I changed my name.

About three quarters of my friends and relatives have made a valiant attempt to use my 'new' name. The other quarter either does not discuss it, or have stated they will continue to call me by my 'old' name because it is too tough to change. I bear no ill will to those who refuse to change but appreciate all those who have participated.

"What's in a name?" asked one of my friends.

I believe there are complex issues afoot and when one changes one's name it is not just the name that is important, but also the reasons behind it.

I am grateful to John who has made a gallant effort to call me Carolann. He admits that at times it is very awkward, but he laughs and says he has gained a new wife without a divorce.

My sons did not dispute my name change. "It doesn't affect me as you'll always be Mum," said one.

What would Edna have thought?

Dissent came from Ian, my adoptive brother. I informed one of my adoptive cousins, prior to enlightening Ian. It was untimely that another relative clued him up before I did.

Ian was shocked and definitely not happy. I should have

discussed my name change with him before I told anyone else, but I have to admit I was reticent because I knew he would not appreciate what I intended to do. I heard he thought I had been disloyal to our parents. As they are both deceased I did not see a problem, but Ian looked at it from their point of view.

I have attempted to understand Ian's feelings and have come to the following conclusion: He was taken aback by my name change as I had years to think about it, but he had not. He did not understand my perspective because he was not aware of adoptive issues, even though he grew up with an adopted sister.

I had always been Ian's sister and the fact I'd had another name and identity beforehand had never entered his mind. Ultimately, we had a one on one discussion and put it behind us. He and every one in his family call me Jean.

I sign emails and cards depending on whether the recipient calls me Jean or Carolann. I guess I am being 'a people pleaser', a tag often applied to adoptees. It's almost like having a split personality. Am I Carolann today or Jean? Someday I am going to make a mistake.

I started life with one identity but that was taken away. Currently, living with two names makes little difference to the confusion I have already experienced as an adoptee.

I did not make the decision lightly or quickly. A positive facet is the ease with which I answer to Carolann. And I always feel happy when I hear someone use it. I guess I feel validated. Even though the change brought some difficulties, I think I did the right thing for me.

34

Holidays and Celebrations

Understand that you will always have one person
on whom you can depend-yourself.
– Sonya Friedman

2008

John and I spent a week on Norfolk Island early in the year and enjoyed the fantastic scenery, history, shops and fresh seafood.

My birth cousin, Annette [Uncle Alf's daughter], asked John and me to her combined sixtieth birthday and wedding anniversary celebration. The party was held in Ipswich at her son's attractive new residence.

I met more birth relations, including Annette's children, husband Merv, sister-in-law, and seven more cousins.

Towards the end of the night we laughed hysterically at a skit in which one of the male guests dressed up as a stripper. He danced to traditional stripper music and played up to Merv, who had been blindfolded on a chair in the middle of the group. Needless to say, he was not impressed when the blindfold was removed.

In spring, John, Louis the poodle, and I departed on a caravan trip to Sydney where we stayed at Sheralee Caravan Park in Rockdale.

We visited Mary and we took Louis and her dogs for a walk in a huge park nearby. She asked us to dinner and we had a good time.

One day John, Mary, and I drove to Wollongong, and ate fish and chips by the sea. After lunch we made an impromptu visit to a local orchid show where Mary bought a plant. Mary and I performed a 'sister act' that day because we had unknowingly worn almost identical black sandals.

John and I visited my birth father, Cyril's, grave at the Macquarie Park Cemetery Lane Cove. We phoned ahead to administration to find the grave location and successfully navigated Sydney's chaotic highways and tunnels.

John drove slowly through the deserted cemetery while I scanned the numbers. I found the right row and John stayed in the car with Louis [dogs were not allowed] as I strolled up and down searching. My heart rate sped up and I started to shake when I could not find Cyril's grave.

John spoke to a groundsman working nearby, who explained some of the graves were unmarked, and advised us how to locate them. Eventually I found the unmarked grave, and took some photographs.

On the 3rd May 2009, John and I celebrated our fortieth wedding anniversary. On a fine autumn morning our friends and relatives arrived to partake of catered luncheon in a marquee erected on the front lawn overlooking the bay.

Our guests arrived laden with gifts for which we were very thankful and we had a great day almost like another wedding day.

Two families from my birth family attended included Leanne and her husband, Brad, and daughter, Carla and Leanne's second cousin, Rory, and his wife, Marlene. Rory, of course, was also my second cousin.

Coincidentally, John and Rory had attended Gatton Agricultural College although in different years. On one occasion John and I met Rory and his wife Marlene, at a Gatton College Old Boys reunion. Life is full of strange coincidences.

My adoptive cousin, Don, was surprised to see Rory at our celebration, because he had been Don's boss in the Nambour Primary Industries Department for years. Don also attended Gatton Agricultural College, in the same years as John and was the go between, or instigator, of John and my meeting in 1967.

We always wished to visit Japan so John and I decided to accompany Andrew and Akiko on their yearly visit to Akiko's hometown, Inyuama, on the island of Honshu.

We flew to Japan in October 2009 and arrived at Nagoya Airport. We strolled to the Centrair Hotel, ordered a light dinner, then had an early night. In two days we would meet up with Andrew and Akiko.

The next morning, John and I boarded the airport train for a one and a half hour journey. Akiko's mother, Naoko, met us at Inyuama Station and drove us to our hotel where we would stay for ten days. We had an interesting attempt at conversation, with mirthful results, because John and I could utter only a few sentences in Japanese and Naoko spoke little English.

We spent time with Andrew, Akiko and her family who showed us impeccable hospitality. On one occasion Akiko's parents, Naoko and Misao, hired a larger car so the six of could travel together to the picturesque mountain town of Gero.

We duly arrived and discovered Naoke and Misao had booked a private room for lunch in the resort, apparently a common occurrence in Japan. Akiko and Andrew opened the bamboo screens on the glass walls so we could overlook a stream with a mountainous backdrop.

We ate a traditional meal in relaxing surroundings then John, Andrew, and Misao took an onsen [hot mineral bath in the nude] in another part of the resort. Naoke had a rest while Akiko and I explored the shopping centre under the restaurant. It was such a pleasure to unite our families in such beautiful surroundings.

35

A Blissful Birth

If you are facing in the right direction,
all you have to do is keep on walking
in order to reach your dreams.
– Wolfgang Riebe

2010

John and I became proud grandparents at 10.00pm on the 28th April. Kerryn gave birth to a baby girl after a labour of only four hours. The ecstatic parents, Chris and Kerryn, named their daughter Kate Jenna.

Kerryn's parents and John and I were invited into the birth suite at Selangor Private Hospital, immediately after Kate's birth. Happiness radiated because the new baby was perfect in every way and the room filled with love for the new arrival.

We celebrated with a glass of champagne and took Kate's first photos. An hour later the staff asked all the new grandparents to leave as Chris and Kerryn needed privacy and would hopefully get some sleep.

Chris and Kerryn were exceedingly proud of their perfect little daughter. Needless to say, John and I were over the moon to be grandparents and welcomed our little granddaughter with all the usual flowers and gifts.

The day after her birth the four grandparents arrived back at the hospital for a second look. That was the first time I held little Kate. I was a tad nervous, as she was so tiny, but filled with love and wonder at her perfection.

From my point of view, as an adoptee, having a granddaughter is extra special as Kate is connected to my feminine genealogy. As time passed, it was clear that the drawing gene has been passed down from Edna to another generation. Kate, who is now three years old, loves to draw. As a two year-old, she drew the family cat, Mia, and her special cuddly toy, Eyore. Her mother framed them. She attends a childcare centre for three days a week and always puts serious effort into her paintings and collages.

In June 2011, John, Louis the poodle, and I departed on a caravan trip to Cooktown. We travelled up the east coast for three weeks until we reached Innisfail where Tev lives.

We booked into a caravan park for five days to spend time with Tev. He was still recovering from a very nasty, life-threatening, type of cancer called mantle cell lymphoma. The previous year he had been through a horrific ordeal, most of it was spent in and out of hospitals. Ultimately he received a blood transplant that his body accepted.

We departed Innisfail and travelled north to Cairns where once again we booked into a caravan park. We indulged in sightseeing and visited adoptive and birth relatives.

On the journey home, we stopped in Innisfail to spend more time with Tev. He had scanned all the old family photos and I was thrilled when he presented me with a computer disk. We used my laptop and looked at them quickly. Most of them I had never seen before so I looked forward to studying them closely at home to gain more insight into the life of my maternal birth family.

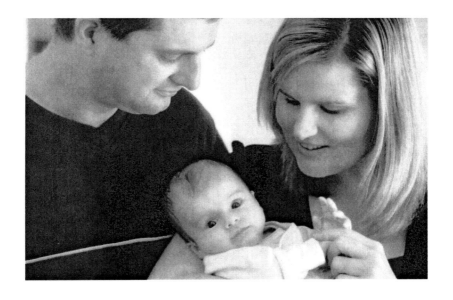

Chris (left) and Kerryn with their daughter, Kate Jenna, (Carolann's granddaughter) in 2010. Photographer: Helen Creagh.

36

Poignant Family Photos

*To achieve purity of mind, one should cultivate constant
awareness by being mindful all the time. One should
remain always aware of one's thoughts.*
– Swami Rama

2012

Late on a fine winter afternoon, I gazed through the glass doors
of my study at a reflected sunset. The sea and sky glowed with
splashes of pink and mauve streaked with silver.

After some minutes my attention was drawn to the shelf
above my desk stacked with computer disks and I remembered
the disk of family photos I had received from Tev in 2011.
Almost a year had passed since our get together.

I inserted the disk into my laptop and downloaded. I
noticed Tev had written messages. Sadness settled in my heart
as I saw another life unfold before me.

The first photo was of a young Edna with long dark curly
hair, dressed in an elegant outfit. I could not believe how much
I resembled her.

The next photo showed a young Edna smiling happily as
she posed in an attractive slacks suit.

The next image was of Edna standing on a beach at Coolum
in the 1940s. She looked happy as her long wavy hair lifted in
the breeze; in another image Edna reclined on a beach towel in
her swimming costume.

A number of photos showed Edna with Tev as a young boy.
They were dressed for formal outings; in some photos Edna had
placed her arm lovingly around Tev's shoulders and in others
held his hand; a very young Tev in the cottage at Ormiston.

I noted in one image Tev mentioned it was the first Christmas he could remember; the lounge room in the cottage decorated with tinsel for Christmas; a decorated Christmas tree; Tev, a child, as he opened his Christmas presents; I noted Tev on his way to the Ormiston State School.

An image of Edna at sixteen showed her with a group of friends. Her dark wavy hair was shoulder length. She wore a fancy striped swimming costume and held a pretty umbrella.

Another image was of Edna, as a young teenager, riding a horse; an older Edna dressed in jodhpurs; Edna at nineteen, striding along a city street, dressed to the hilt; Edna aged twenty-one in a stunning profile portrait with an immaculate 1930s hairstyle; Edna and Tev posed with a group of relatives.

My maternal [birth] grandmother, Martha, on a chair in her old fashioned kitchen, slippers on her feet, playing her piano accordion; Edna in the bush at Ormiston with her arms around Tev and her niece, Susan; Tev and his cousin, Regina, playing together during childhood. [Regina is a birth cousin I have never met.] Edna posed with two female friends in a spotless 1940s kitchen.

Edna's love for Tev during his childhood was quite apparent. He was always well dressed and so was she.

I decided Edna had been a good mother to Tev and would have been to me too. Tears ran down my cheeks. I grabbed a handful of tissues and had a good cry. I had been born to Edna, I belonged with her, but fate had separated us. Our likeness was mirrored in the photos.

Up to the present day, I had seen few photos of Edna as a young woman and my uncanny likeness to her, in the photos, created an especially poignant experience.

In the past I had not taken my resemblance to Edna seriously although Tev had often mentioned it. We were different ages, Edna being thirty years older, but now as I compared our young photos, I was bowled over by our similarities.

It was one of the happiest and saddest moments of my journey.

My guilt was severe. I had a good life with my adoptive parents. How could I wish for another life when they did everything for me? I was so confused.

I called out to John. He was busy and a little reluctant but came anyway. As we viewed the photos of Edna's life, it was apparent John, too, was affected and we both shed tears. It seemed we were attending her funeral. The photos had stirred up a sadness I had not anticipated.

Recently Tev found Selena, his American half-sister. Tev's birth father returned to America in 1944 and married soon after. His wife gave birth to Selena, but during her childhood her parents separated and lost touch with each other.

Selena recently went online to search for information about her father and his family. She also mentioned her father had an illegitimate son, in Australia, nicknamed Tevy. Tev saw the blog and contacted her and they have stayed in touch.

I emailed Tev and explained the sadness I experienced when I saw the old family photos. He said he knew exactly what I meant, because he had experienced the same emotion, when he saw photos of his American birth family. It was a life of which he had not been part. He and I had been excluded from our birth parents' lives and grieved for them.

Tev had missed out on having a father, an event not easily reconciled. The effects of the Second World War are readily apparent in his story, a story that has been played out many times.

37

Adoption and Healing

Only courageous people allow themselves to be vulnerable.
– Nancy Verrier

2012

Apparently writing about painful memories can be cathartic and forms a very important role in psychological healing. A memoir gives an author the opportunity to speak and revisit her topic.

Writing is extremely important for adoptees as it provides an opportunity to those who were prevented from speaking in the past. I decided to give it a try.

I have attempted to demonstrate two parallels I have lived since early childhood. They are my 'adoptive' versus my 'biological' or 'what if' life. In adulthood, they have often run on separate tracks and the separation is even more evident when one considers most members of my birth family are unacquainted with members of my adoptive family or in-laws.

Adoptive issues have taken up a large portion of my life and I am sure they will continue to do so because researchers acknowledge adoption as a 'lifetime event'.

I have searched for many years for important pieces of information – 'where did I come from?' and 'whom did I come from?'

Through writing I have experienced new levels of peace and stability. I was required to delve deep and managed to straighten out my thoughts to create a coherent story. I gained more understanding of my issues, acceptance of my role as an adoptee, and I am now cognisant of the fact that nothing can change the past.

I have acquired more empathy for my birth mother's issues but I do not think I will ever totally recover from being relinquished.

I am able to feel love for everyone connected with my adoption and have more understanding of the formerly unfathomable reasons for my anger.

I have participated in loads of counselling, from a variety of counsellors, starting when I was thirty-five. I have evolved through different stages of grief that were necessary before I could accept my adoption.

Previously I have mentioned adoptees may suffer from depression and anxiety, and I certainly have. During a psychological assessment, I was diagnosed with Generalised Anxiety Disorder and I am on medication. Would I, if I had never been relinquished?

The Belmont Cognitive Behaviour Therapy Unit runs a course in Cognitive Behaviour Therapy at the Belmont Private Hospital and I have taken it twice.

The original course was intensive as it ran for one month, five days a week, with one day off per week to consolidate new skills.

The second course ran for three weeks and during that time I used the option to stay in the hospital as a patient. As the saying goes, knowledge is power, so the course was highly beneficial. Participants also received one on one counselling with counsellors and their doctor.

The course is a comprehensive and intense program for anxiety and depression. The following broad topics are covered in detail: anxiety, depression and anger management, cognitive re-structuring, communication and social skills, stress management, and general life management skills.

Recently I attended a two-day workshop for adoptees, and a regional meeting for members of the adoption triad, organised by Post Adoption Support Queensland. PASQ is a service of the Benevolent Society.

The Benevolent Society, Australia's first charity, has cared for vulnerable people, families, and communities for nearly two hundred years. Established in 1813, they are an independent, non-religious organisation, working to provide positive change in response to society's needs.

The Benevolent Society provides a team of professionals who run Post Adoption Support Queensland (PASQ). They are trained to best support the community in working with issues unique to adoption. They provide face-to-face counselling, telephone support and counselling, and therapeutic groups and themed workshops. They visit regional areas, to inform adoptees of new laws and current support systems, and help participants with research and reunions. PASQ promotes a sense of belonging and encourage discussion, between members of the adoption triad.

PASQ visited Redland Bay earlier this year and John and I attended with approximately twelve others from the adoption triad. I found it beneficial as it provided the chance to discuss adoption issues with others who shared similar experiences, and PASQ provides a safe environment for these discussions.

The Benevolent Society headquarters is located at 9 Wilson Street West End, Brisbane, where I recently attended a two-day Therapeutic 'Sense of Self' workshop.

The workshop for adoptees encouraged the learning of techniques based on cognitive behaviour therapy. The techniques increased ones sense of personal self, promoted relaxation, reduced anxiety, and helped one cope with stress.

The workshop also provided the opportunity for open discussion between members of the adoptee group. The counsellors promoted a sense of belonging a feeling that is extremely important for adoptees because we are a minority group.

Jigsaw Queensland is another support group of which I am a member. In the past I have attended meetings at their headquarters in New Farm. I have also completed a course specifically for members of the adoption triad. I found all of the above to be beneficial.

In aid of healing, I have found it advantageous to read a number of self-help adoption based manuals. Understanding oneself is extremely important to the healing process and the more one reads the better. I also found it helpful to read the personal accounts of other adoptees.

It is spring and from my study I gaze on a sea that sparkles while a slight northerly breeze whips up white tops on the wavelets that roll gently to shore.

My memoir is finished and I know I am going to miss it. It has become an old friend.

I have noticed my anger on certain adoptive issues has greatly diminished through this journey. Although, just today, a stab of anger jabbed me when I pondered the absence of my birth father's name in the Department of Families' records.

I am sure some adoptive issue or comment from others related to adoption will continue to upset me at times. Nevertheless, writing about my feelings has put many issues into perspective and I recommend it. I accept the fact some issues will always linger and moments of anger may surface from time to time.

If I had my time over would I take such a journey? Of course I would. I would rather know the facts than be kept in the dark.

The following is a little adoptee humour from two adoption researchers, Victor Groza and Karen Rosenberg:

"How often does an adoptee change a light bulb?"

"Never because they are used to being kept in the dark."

If I had remained ignorant I would not have met many amazing members of my birth family and my life would be poorer for that.

I accept my adoption now, although deep down the hurt still lingers. I no longer feel like a victim, and attempt to see myself as the recipient of a variety of interesting experiences as I balance out the painful side of this truth.

Not every adoptee will have the outcome I have had. Some may not have the opportunity to meet their birth family. Some are forced to live with 'hurtful officialdom' in the form of a veto that prevents a reunion. For others, a reunion is prevented by the untimely death of a birth family member. Some do not have supportive adoptive parents and others are never told the truth. And not everyone would have the wonderful support

I have received from my husband, John. I am grateful for his help and understanding.

I have been extremely fortunate to complete my journey and was privileged that most members of my birth family welcomed me into their lives.

I am lucky a good family adopted me. My adoptive parents remained in a stable marriage so I had a sound basis for childhood growth and happiness. My parents were mentally stable and well able to focus care upon their children. They were not overly indulgent in alcohol or anything else.

I have read that the relationship of an adoptee with his or her adoptive mother is of extreme importance so I am thankful for my adoptive mother, who was a genuinely lovely person and we developed a close, loving relationship.

I would judge the outcome of my journey as excellent, but I am amongst the lucky. I have people in my life who care and surely that is one of life's most precious gifts.

But still – no one would choose to be adopted.

Note:
My memoir is focused on my adoptive situation as an infant adoptee. I had no knowledge whatsoever of my identity. Perhaps older children from abusive families who are removed and placed in foster homes, or children in orphanages, may wish to be adopted.

It is crucial to remember that when an older child is adopted he or she would have knowledge of his or her identity. They would most likely retain their Christian names and have other family knowledge. Depending on their age, an older adoptee may also know their ancestors' names and nationality. In that way, they differ greatly from an adoptee, such as myself, who was placed for adoption as an infant. I believe, to remove the identity of a human being is inhumane.

Sadly, on August 17 2013, my birth brother, Tev, passed away peacefully in the palliative care section of the Gordonvale hospital. John and I flew to Cairns to attend his funeral with Tev's son Alex, daughter-in-law Aya and granddaughter Sarah.

Tev (Carolann's birth brother) in the 1960s.

Carolann with her birth brother Tev on the day they met in 1992.
Photographer: John Dowding.

Tev (Carolann's birth brother) on the right with his son Alex.

From left: Lachlan, Chris and Andrew (Carolann's sons) in 1982.
Koala Photographics.

Carolann (right) with her birth cousin, Leanne, in 2008.
Photographer: John Dowding.

Carolann (right) with her birth cousin, Leanne, and birth aunt,
Alma Ethel, (front) in 2003. Photographer: Brad Livermore.

Carolann and John in 1992. Photographer: Judith Gordon.

Carolann (left) with her birth sister Mary on the day they met
in 2007. Photographer: John Dowding.

Carolann (right)
with her birth
sister, Mary, at
Windang Beach
New South
Wales in 2009.
Photographer:
John Dowding.

Joanne and Lachlan
(Carolann's son) in
1992. Cleveland High
School Photographer.

Lachlan (Carolann's son) graduated in 1999 with a Bachelor of Information Technology (Computing Science) with Distinction. Photographer: Ray Rapinette.

Chris (Carolannn's son) graduated in 1994 with a Bachelor of Engineering (Civil) with Honors 2A. Elite Photographics.

Kerryn and Chris (Carolann's son) with officiating priest in 2001.
Photographer: John Reyment.

Andrew (Carolann's son) graduated in 2001 with a Bachelor of
Information Technology (Computing Science). Location, Nishikamo,
Kyoto, Japan. Photographer: Akiko Kojima.

From Left: Joanne, Belinda, Kerryn, Akiko, Andrew (Carolann's son),
Chris, Shinya and Lachlan in 2005 at, Sirromet, Mount Cotton.
Wings Photography.

John and Carolann cutting their anniversary cake in 2009.
Photographer: Lesley Bullen.

John and Carolann's wedding party forty years later!
From left: Ian (adoptive brother), Graeme, John, Carolann, Christina
and Carol (John's sister). Photographer: Lesley Bullen.

Carolann and John with their sons, from left, Lachlan, Andrew
and Chris at their fortieth wedding anniversary celebration in 2009.
Photographer: Lesley Bullen.

Carolann (right) graduated in 2003 with a Bachelor of Fine Art.
Griffith University Photographer.

Carolann (left) with her friend, DiAnne, in 2010 who she met in 1953
at Redland Bay Primary School. Photographer: John Dowding.

Enjoying the hospitality of the Kojimas (Akiko's parents) in Japan
in 2009. From left: Akiko, John, Carolann, Andrew and Shinya.
Photographer: Misao Kojima.

Carolann with her granddaughter Kate in 2012.
Photographer: Elle McDonald.

Carolann in 2011 with her birth brother, Tev, in Innisfail.
Photographer: John Dowding.

Carolann with her adoptive brother, Ian, in 2013 at Redland Bay.
Photographer: John Dowding.

From left: Lachlan, Jo, Akiko, Andrew, Kerryn and Chris.
Photographer: Lesley Bullen.

The Dowding family in 2011. From left at back: Chris, Kerryn,
Andrew and Lachlan. In front: John and Carolann holding Kate.
Photographer: Ray Rapinette.

Kate (Carolann's granddaughter)
aged seventeen months in 2011.
Photographer: Ray Rapinette.

Carolann with her birth mother, Edna, in 2002.
Photographer: John Dowding.

John (Jack) Joseph Carlyle (Carolann's paternal birth grandfather) with his wife Ethel Mary in 1926.

Edna (Carolann's birth mother) aged eighty-seven in 2004. Photographer: C. Dowding.

References

Glazebrook, Collette. (2007). *Facing the Fears*. Salisbury: Boolarong Press.

Georgeff, Diana. (2007). *Delinquent Angel*. Sydney: Random House.

Groza, Victor.; Rosenberg, Karen. (1998). *Clinical and Practice Issues in Adoption*. Westport: Bergin and Gravey.

Hunt, C. (2006). Post Adoption Helping Skills Workshop. Brisbane: Jigsaw Queensland.

Lifton, Betty Jean. (1994). *Journey of the Adopted Self – A Quest for Wholeness*. United States of America: Basic Books, A Member of the Perseus Books Group.

Lifton, Betty Jean. (2009). *Lost and Found: The Adoption Experience*. United States of America: University of Michigan Press.

Morganti, Anthony. (2011). *Quotes to Enrich Life and Spirit – From Buddha through Gandhi to Zen*. Smashwords Edition.

Riebe, Wolfgang. (2010). *100 Quotations To Make You Think*. Mind Power Publications at Smashwords.

Verrier, Nancy Newton. (1993) *The Primal Wound: Understanding the Adopted Child*. Baltimore: Gateway Press Inc.

Verrier, Nancy Newton. (2003) *Coming Home to Self: The Adopted Child Grows Up*. Baltimore: Gateway Press Inc.

Wagner, Jenny. (1974) *The Bunyip of Berkeley's Creek*. Victoria: Penguin Group (Australia).

Other Prose @ IP

Yellowcake Summer, by Guy Salvidge
ISBN 9781922120625, AU$33

You Only Want Me for My Mind, by John Rynn with John Corrigan
ISBN 9781922120601, AU$30

Sawdust, by Deborah Kay & Barry Levy
ISBN 9781922120373, AU$33

Sexual Abuse Survivor's Handbook, by John Saunders
ISBN 9781922120564, AU$30

Art from Adversity: A Life with Bipolar, by Anne Naylor
ISBN 9781922120113, AU$33

The Beast Without, by Christian Baynes
ISBN 9781922120434, AU$33

Frenchmans Cap: Story of a Mountain, by Simon Kleinig
ISBN 9781922120052, AU$33

Memories of Dr Shinichi Suzuki, by Lois Shepheard
ISBN 9781922120137, AU$30

The Terrorist, by Barry Levy
ISBN 9781922120076, AU$33

Blood, by Peter Kay
ISBN 9781922120038, AU$33

The Rag Boiler's Daughter, by Lois Shepheard
ISBN 9781921869389, AU$30

For the latest from IP, please visit us online at
http://ipoz.biz/Store/Store.htm
or contact us by phone/fax on 61 7 3324 9319
or sales@ipoz.biz

0 1341 1571646 3

CPSIA information can be obtained at www.ICGtesting.com
Printed in the USA
LVOW06s2149300614

392435LV00001B/210/P

9 781922 12066